FUTURE
SYSTEMS
DEYAN SUDJIC

FUT
SYST
DEYAN

URE

EMS

SUDJIC

Φ

Small objects are instant gratification. Rather than waiting for years to see your baby, you can see results in a matter of weeks Amanda Levete

ALESSI 300

Le Caprice

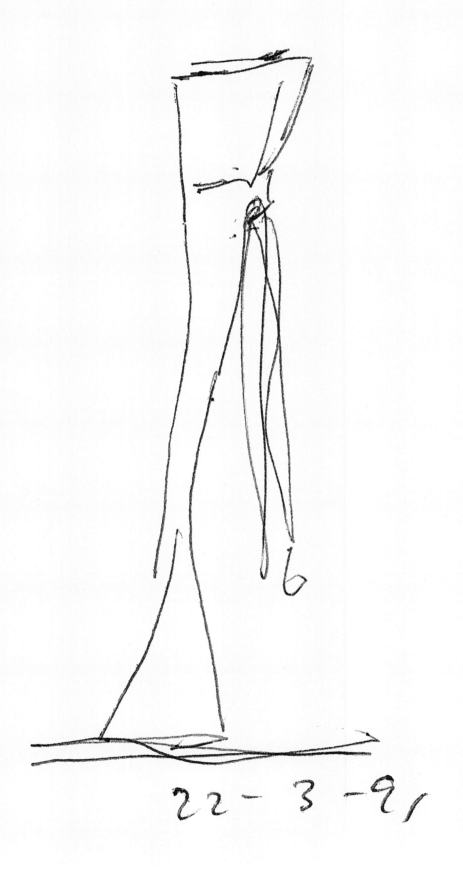

22 - 3 - 91

**188 Champagne Bucket,
cast aluminium, 1991.**

CHAMPAGNE
BUCKET
188

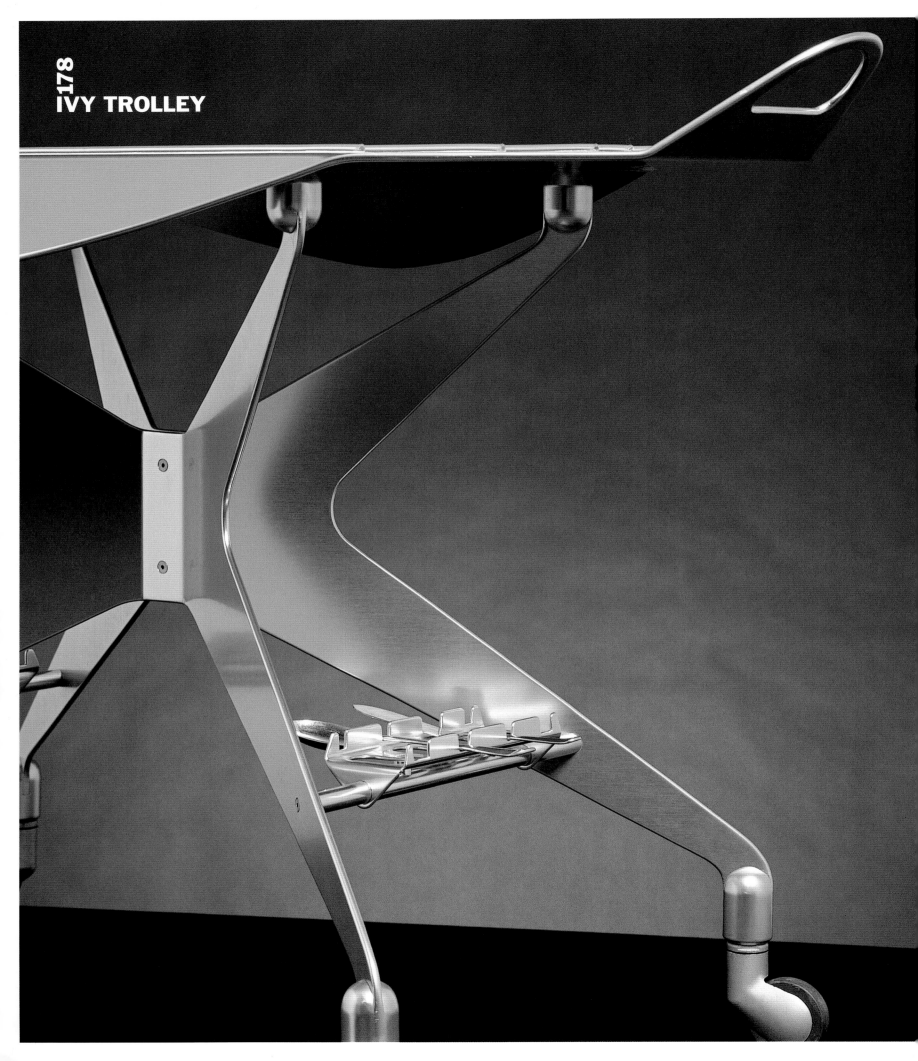

rnesto Rogers, a partner in the Milanese studio Banfi, Belgiojoso, Peressutti and Rogers (BBPR), once famously suggested that it should be possible to deduce, simply from looking at a spoon, what kind of city the culture that manufactured it would build. In fact, since Rogers' heyday in the 1950s, architects have concentrated their attention not so much on spoons as on chairs, the one object above all others that so many seem determined to master. They are motivated, consciously or unconsciously, by the hope of replicating the achievements of Marcel Breuer, or those of Charles and Ray Eames. Breuer's once-in-a-lifetime flash of intuition about the load-bearing potential of the tubular steel used for the handlebars of the bicycle that he was pedalling around the streets of Dessau, served to produce the epoch-defining Wassily tubular steel chair. And ever since, the ability to design at least one truly convincing chair has been seen as representing a crucial measure of architectural achievement. Even more impressive than Breuer's creation was that of Charles and Ray Eames, who worked with moulded plywood and steel castings, producing a series of chairs that still look as fresh now as they did almost half a century ago when they were first manufactured.

The implication contained in Rogers's words is that the design of the industrially produced object is part of a single continuum, stretching all the way to architecture and urbanism. But the last fifty years have in fact seen a widening gulf between architects – who operate at the scale of a building – and industrial designers, who work on the artefacts that shape the internal landscape, most of which can sit on a table top. A chair is not in fact a miniature building, even if it might reflect some parallel thinking about form, materials and space. And the design of taps and sanitary fittings, door handles and lamps, let alone the glasses and the tableware that were once the exclusive preserve of architects, at least in the early days

178 Ivy Trolley, anodized
aluminium plate, 1990.

143 Chaise Longue,
prototype, 1986.

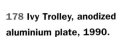

203 Superbus, concept
project, 1993.

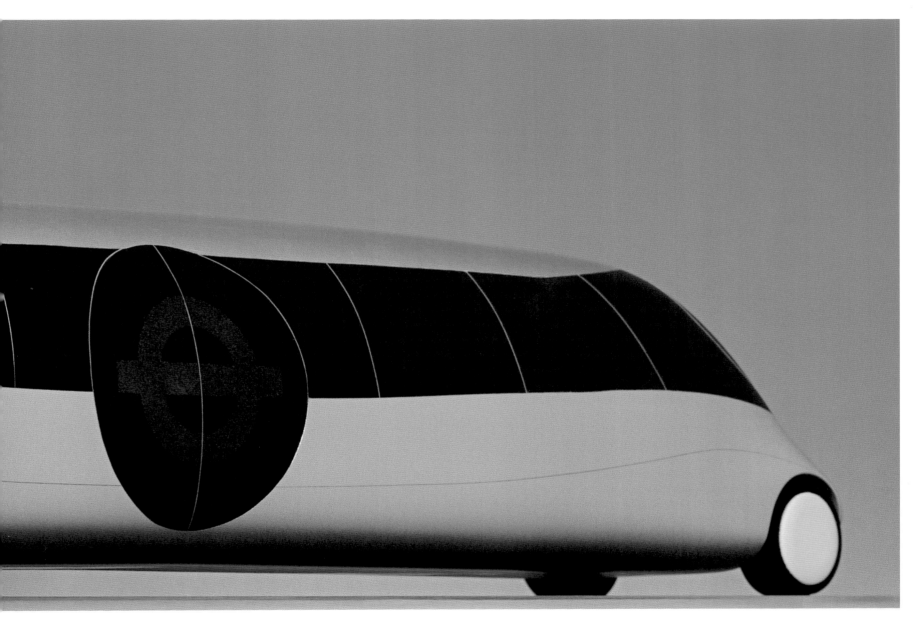

of modernism, is a task that has been taken over by others. These objects are now shaped mostly by specialist designers with a sensibility that is distinctively different in its priorities from that of architects.

Yet the professional division between architecture and design remains fluid. This is not least because so many furniture and product designers in Italy, a country that still sets the agenda for industrial design, were trained as architects. And paradoxically, the more successful they are at designing products, the greater is their continuing desire to build architecture. Architects, on the other hand, in part as their celebrity status has grown, find themselves increasingly in demand by certain manufacturers who are looking, in the most banal cases, for a signature to apply to what is usually an anonymous object in the hope of differentiating it from its generic competitors. But more positively, sometimes they are searching for a wider range of thinking and a more contextual approach. The result is a category of objects that is midway between utilitarian, anonymous equipment, and what used to be called 'applied art'.

Future Systems were interested in exploring definitions of design beyond architecture from an early stage. It is an interest that comes naturally to the kind of architect who enjoys spending hours poring over manufacturers' catalogues, looking for anonymous objects for inspiration, as well as for the chance to use them in new and unfamiliar ways. But Future Systems have also worked on the design of small objects as a

186
CARAVAN

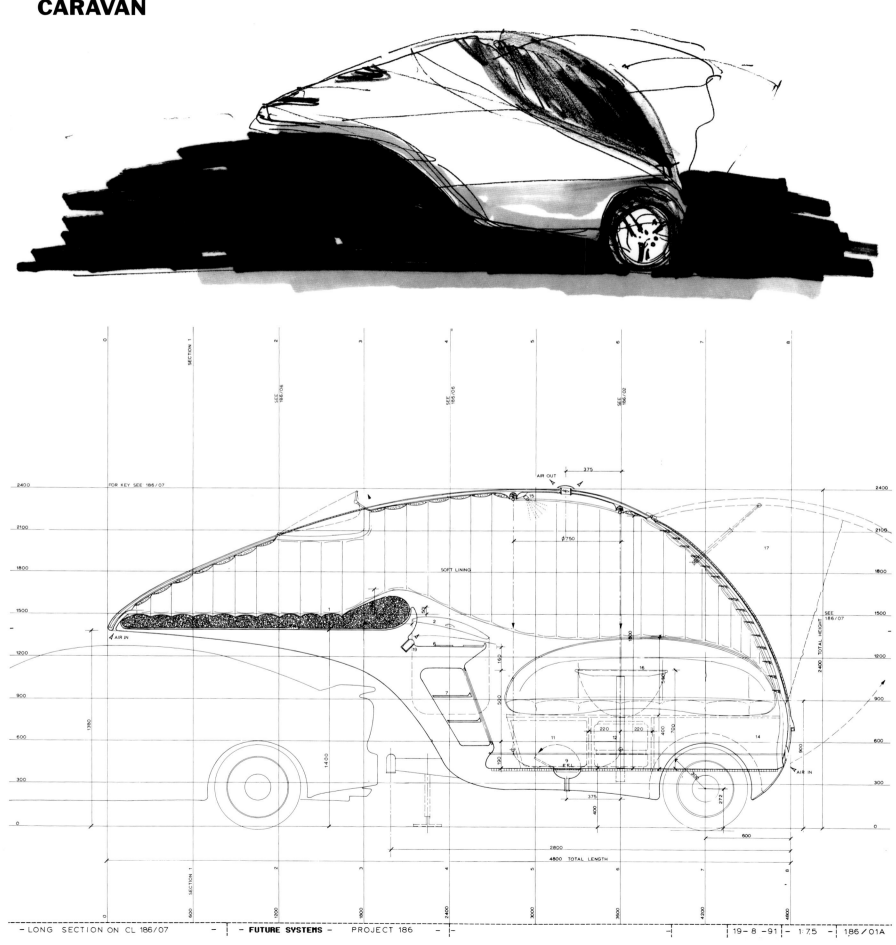

part of their architectural projects. 'We tried to integrate the furniture into the walls at first,' says Kaplicky:

> but doing that eventually leads to the question of what is the interior in a home. An interest in objects came late to me. The early interiors that we designed had no furniture in them; you just dreamed of a soft bed in a soft room. But in the end I had to think about it. You need something else apart from Le Corbusier or Eames.

Several of Future Systems' domestic projects have involved designing and manufacturing one-off tables, beds and storage units. It was a useful way to avoid the predictability of the conventional architectural choices that has resulted at times in every office lobby being equipped with Mies's Barcelona chair, and every desk lit by an Anglepoise lamp.

> 'As an architect you can't prescribe what people will use. Of course, you try to make suggestions. But it's like having all your clothes from the same designer. You can have the shoes, and the dress, but if you have the handbag as well, then suddenly, it's all over.'

From these beginnings, Kaplicky and Levete started to work on individual objects that were anything but invisible. In 1991 they designed a champagne bucket for the Caprice restaurant – whose co-owner at the time, Jeremy King, also commissioned Future Systems to design a house for his family. For the same restaurant, they conceived a carefully detailed trolley, fabricated from 6 mm thick anodized aluminium plate, using off-the-peg wheels, and including a little shelf for cutlery. 'It was made by bolting components together, because you can't weld anodized aluminium', Kaplicky explains. They used an anodized finish, which is easier to maintain than steel since it does not rust. Stainless steel would also have been too unyielding and too noisy. Future Systems also worked on a proposal for a coffee jug for the restaurant, with a scale more robust than the domestic cafetière that it would have replaced, and a plastic handle to prevent it from becoming too hot to hold. And there were speculative projects too: a wheeled chaise longue for an exhibition at the Institute of Contemporary Arts in 1988 – produced in response to an invitation to design a chair – a project for a caravan in 1991, to be manufactured in Australia that got as far as prototype stage, and in 1993 a proposal for a London bus.

But the major step towards practising design on the scale of the individual object came when Future Systems were invited by Alessi, the Italian firm specializing in tableware and cutlery, to contribute a design for their tea and coffee project in 2001. Twenty years earlier Alberto Alessi had anticipated in miniature the coming wave of post-modernism by commissioning a selection of soon-to-be-famous architects, ranging from Michael Graves to Robert Venturi, to design silverware sets for his company. This time he wanted to do the same with another generation, and another movement. But in the early years of the twenty-first century, Alessi found it impossible to establish a single architectural language, and opted instead for diversity.

From their initial involvement with the project, Future Systems have established a continuing relationship with Alessi that has led to a wide range of domestic objects – cutlery as well as glassware and china – with the aim of reaching a wider audience than the buyers of their one-off, hammered-silver coffee service. At the same time, they have begun to produce furniture, products and lights for a number of other companies, making design, as distinct from architecture, a significant part of their activities. Levete has also worked for the Venetian glass company, Salviati.

Since then, Future Systems have turned their attention to a range of other objects, even a car. Following in the footsteps of Le Corbusier's experiments in designing a lightweight, petrol-driven vehicle, Kaplicky has worked on an electric-powered, three-seater car, giving it a high, off-the-ground profile, but a relatively wide wheelbase for stability.

'Chairs are the most challenging objects to design,' says Kaplicky.

> You can try all you can to move ahead, but in the 1930s people produced a new world that's never been surpassed. The things that Charlotte Perriand did when she was just twenty-five, or Marcel Breuer did when he was twenty-four, are still modern. I designed chairs in school. They were in wood at first. Then I did a table in steel and wood. They were never very strong. That work was a kind of a private lab. I didn't want to make things myself; I was always designing for other people to make them, but I liked the idea of things being tailored to specific circumstances. For me, ready-made projects have never been so interesting. I didn't like prefab systems, and I was worried by what a world shaped by mechanical mass production really represents.

Kaplicky remains interested in the tactile quality of objects. 'Comfort is hardly talked about, but it's very difficult to get a chair right; the fundamental differences are in the material quality.'

There are parallels in some of Future Systems' designs with their architectural work, particularly in their use of colour, and their interest in sensuous form. In 2005, for example, they designed an ice bucket for a glassware company that is intended for bar-top use. It is shaped to cradle the bottle in a glass basket that will keep the ice closely packed. The glass contains colour gradations that become paler towards the top, in a way that is reminiscent of the facade that they designed for Comme des Garçons in Paris. The first step in designing

186 Caravan, prototype, 1991.

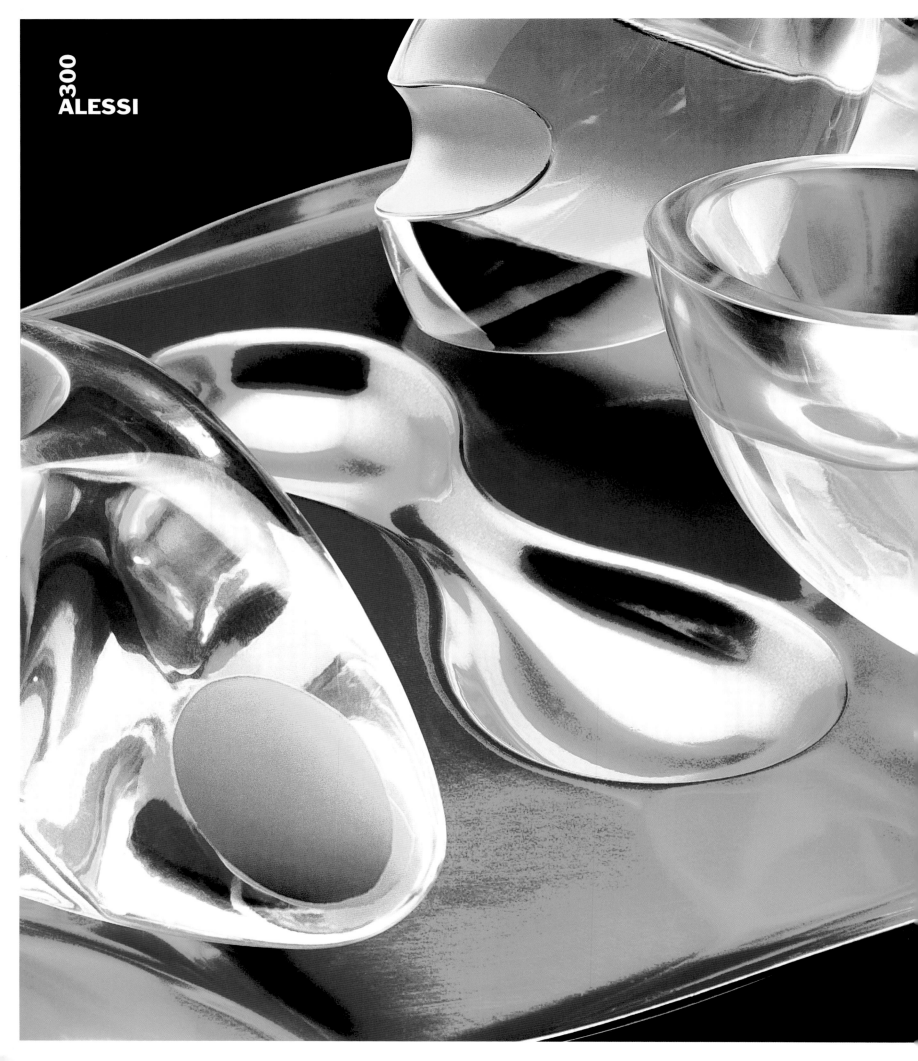

300 **Alessi, Tea and Coffee Set, Pyrex, 2001.**

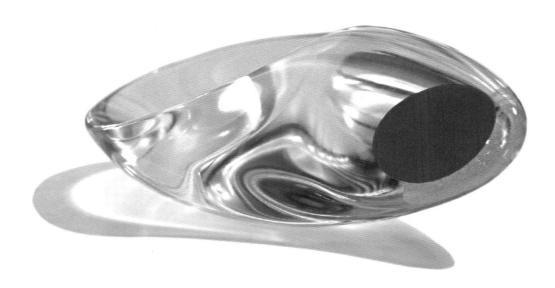

the ice bucket was to model it in Plasticine. That sketch model was then converted into a more precisely shaped and detailed model, which in turn was realized in blown glass, and cut with a flame to create an asymmetric shape.

In 2004 Future Systems designed a light for Fontana Arte that will be available in floor, wall and ceiling versions, with a blown-glass diffuser, a tubular aluminium structure, and a special stainless-steel support to accommodate a stabilizing base at one end and the lamp at the other. Special care was given to the choice of materials. Aluminium was deemed suitable because it could be easily polished up to the mirror finish that the designers wanted to give it.

In the spring of 2005, Levete took part in the ambitious launch in Milan of a range of furniture by a variety of architects and designers working for a new British furniture manufacturer, the somewhat archly named Established and Sons. She took the traditional buttoned-leather Chesterfield sofa as her point of departure, but gave it a free form that bears the same relationship to

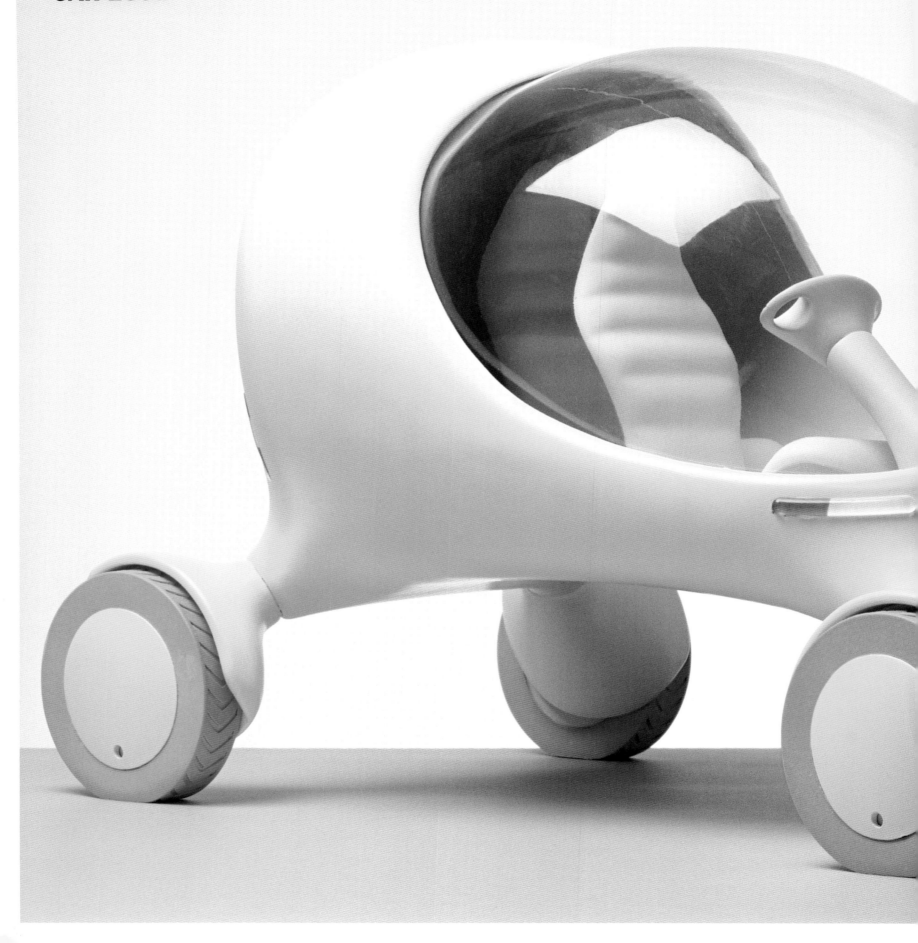

297 **Car 2001, concept project, 2001.**

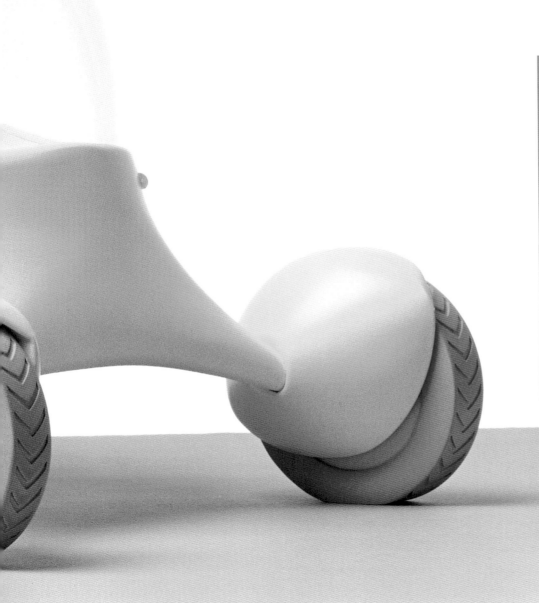

GLASS CHAMPAGNE BUCKET

the conventional sofa as a melting Dalí clock has to the orthodox mantelpiece version.

The Chesterfield was done very quickly for the launch, but afterwards we worked on two versions, the limited-edition piece with a cantilever, and the production version without. We worked on it so quickly that things happened too fast for us to reconsider. It turned out a bit literal, which we were able to work on afterwards.

For Levete, 'small objects are instant gratification. Rather than waiting for years to see your baby, you can see results in a matter of weeks.' She still sees designing furniture as closely related to architecture:

It's about comfort: the same issues, but looser and more liberating. You don't have to worry about keeping the rain out or structural collapse. At the same time, designing furniture does need a similar way of looking at things as architecture, the little ideas inform the big ideas. And the more you do, the more ideas feed off each other.

Levete identifies certain forms and shapes as recurring at different scales in their work, in particular the bean, which has been a generator for buildings as well as objects.

**401 Glass Champagne Bucket,
Moser, 2005.**

Design at the scale of the object has been a challenging but stimulating experience for both Kaplicky and Levete. It has forced them, for instance, to consider the rituals that define the dining table, to look at issues of comfort, and to explore the world from the very different scale of the table top. Alessi even employs a consultant to advise on issues of table etiquette, and despite the apparent freedom that they have brought to shape-making, Future Systems' designs have had to pass that test, as well as those presented by manufacturing techniques.

If a building is like an epic novel, with adequate room for gradual development, and with space for quieter passages, as well as more declamatory ones, a spoon is more of a haiku. And as such, it leaves no room for the designer to hide, or to make a mistake. Everything is visible. Every millimetre needs to be painstakingly considered from every angle. For Future Systems, with their interest in technology, the opportunity to work on mass-produced objects was a chance to get closer to the manufacturing process, in a way that architecture still cannot do.

The challenge represented by the design of cutlery or glassware is not only in the formal inventiveness it requires, but also in the need to consider how big a step to take with redefining each object. There are archetypes to be considered that cannot be abandoned lightly. Future Systems are aware of the issue of time in the design of domestic objects, and the need to move with caution.

A classic cutlery design should still be modern after fifty years. When you're designing a new one, if you go one step forward, it will work; if you take two steps, that can be too much. It moves beyond what people can recognize, or feel comfortable with.

Household objects need to adopt a certain reticence, or to maintain a balance between those objects that are foregrounded, and those that are not. Not everything on the table should adopt the same formal language. Kaplicky cites Adolf Loos's work for the Viennese glass maker Lobmeyer:

He didn't do very much, but what he did do was very strong. He put cross-hatched lines on the base of a simple whisky glass. The effect was like ice, but at the same time it looked as if the glass had always been decorated that way. You wouldn't say it was a Loos glass unless you happened to know he had designed it, but it still looks completely modern 100 years later.

374
FLORA LAMP

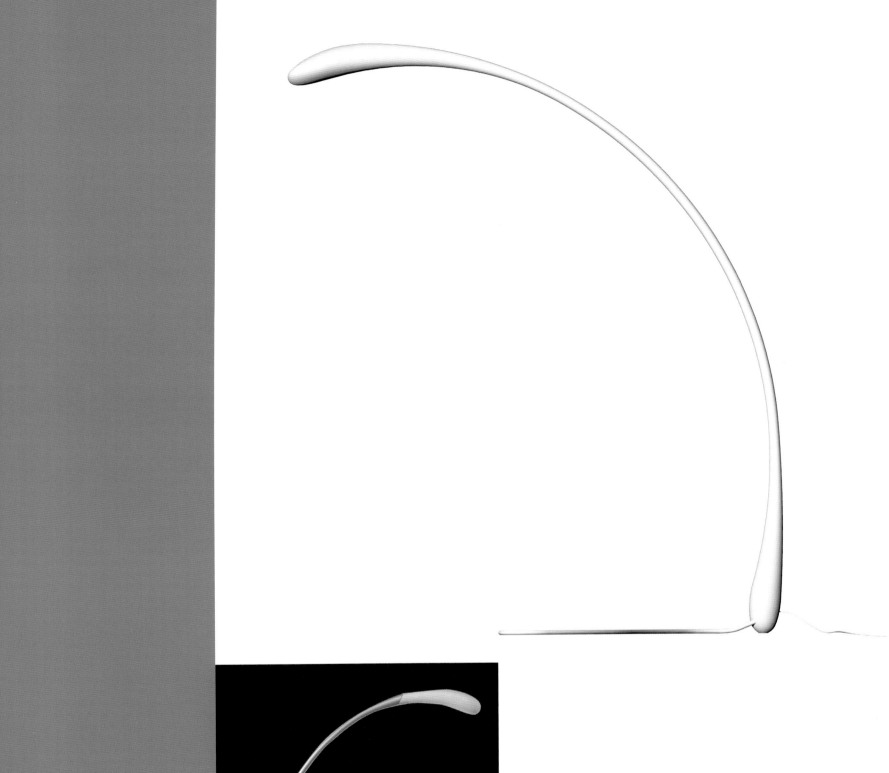

374 **Flora Lamp, aluminium, blown glass and stainless steel, Fontana Arte, 2004.**

Comfort is hardly talked about, but it's very difficult to get a

330 **Swiss Table, concept project, 2002.**

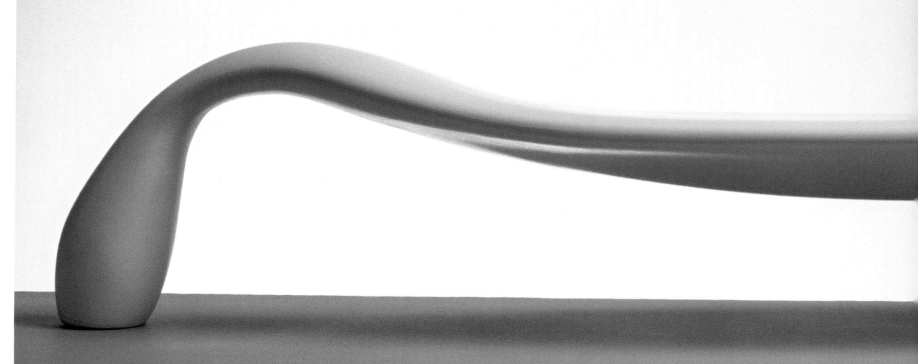

chair right; **thefundamental** differences are in the **material quality** Jan Kaplicky

SWISS TABLE 330

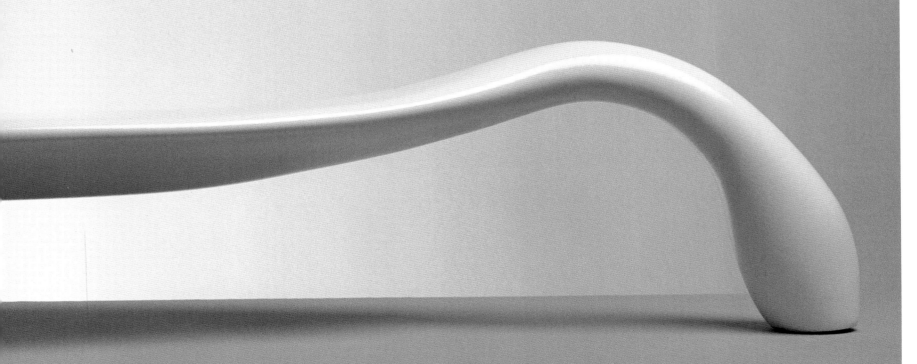

If the traditional rituals that accompany a formal meal are not to be uncomfortably disrupted, a fork needs to look something like a fork, and a wine glass needs to communicate its function, and to let users know if it is intended for red or white wine. But Future Systems' cutlery for Alessi has certainly pushed into fresh territory, with a palette of curved forms, and a clear differentiation between those elements that are handled by the user and the tool that the handle is used to manipulate.

These are objects that tread a delicate line between familiarity and the unusual. 'When I showed some of these objects to people who aren't in the design world, they said that they had never realized that a glass can be self-consciously designed,' says Kaplicky. 'I have to explain to them that an anonymous glass doesn't just come from another planet.'

But the larger question beyond either reinforcing or subverting the archetypes was the shift in scale from design to architecture. 'For some people,' says Kaplicky:

the scale of an object is fascinating; for others, trying to deal with it is painful. An object is not a small building. It is a different problem. Personally, I don't think there is a division between architecture and design. I don't accept it, but an architect has to keep in mind that to design a small object is to reveal your weaknesses in a way that a building does not. Every bolt is visible, and you learn bitter lessons about the detailing of the details. It's a category that simply doesn't exist on a building.

Alessi is one of those unusual companies that is led by its search for a strong creative direction, rather than by conventional ideas about marketing, or the need to keep existing production lines busy. 'Alessi never asked us to look at this material, or use that production technique,' says Kaplicky. 'Once we were selected to do one of the coffee sets, they asked us to work on some cutlery designs, then in the middle of lunch at the factory at Crusinallo in the Italian mountains, Alberto Alessi, suddenly asked, "Why don't you do china, and what about some glass, as well?"' In fact, though it does have an in-house metal-working capability, the company has moved to out-sourced production, working with injection-moulded plastics, and subcontracting the production of its clocks and watches. The cup on which Future Systems was working when I visited their office is made of china and will be made in a variety of sizes. The raw material comes in semi-liquid form, a little stiffer than toothpaste, and is injected into a mould.

The result is a wide range of objects that, while they clearly reflect Future Systems' predilections, do not belong to a single family, and are not intended to form a complete table-top landscape. Perhaps the most striking pieces are the glasses: a set of champagne flutes, red-wine balloons, spirit and white-wine glasses, all

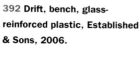

392 Drift, bench, glass-reinforced plastic, Established & Sons, 2006.

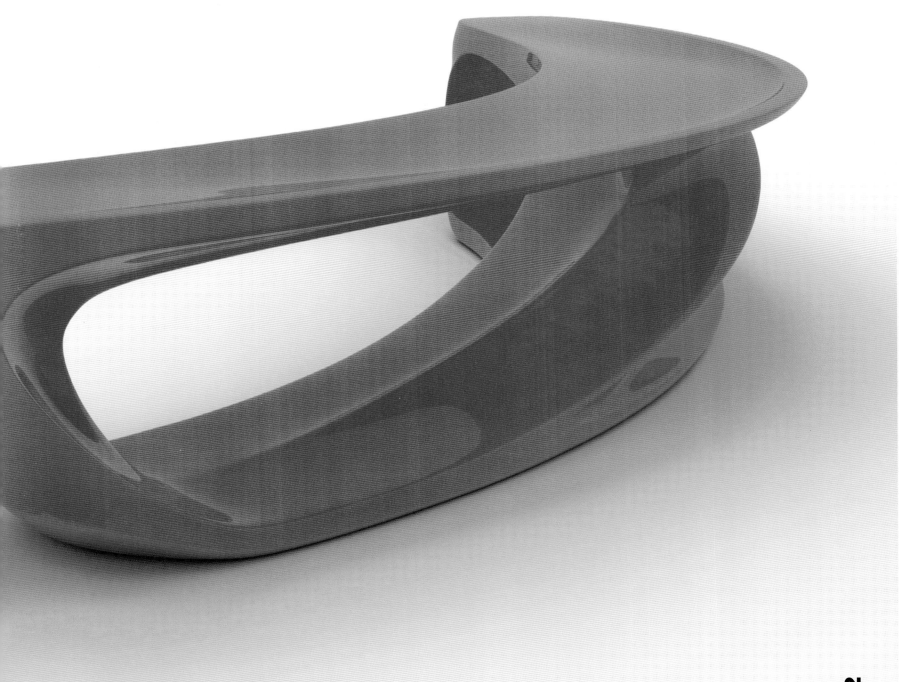

372 Alessi Cutlery, table and airline range, stainless steel and plastic, 2004.

made up of a blown-glass element that sits on a detachable stem, like a flower vase, made in plastic or stainless steel, that can take any one of the four alternative glasses. 'Technically, you might call it primitive,' says Kaplicky.

The glass is blown and cut in a way that my father, who taught glass-making at the Academy of Fine Arts in Prague after the war, would have recognized. Glass is glass: it's a material that is at least 3,000 years old; ceramics are probably 25,000 years old. You can't just experiment for the sake of it. It's enough that you can make a glass without a stem and a base. People always ask about using new materials, but you can still work very well with earth, glass and wood. The question is how you make the way that you use the material new, and that newness is what could lead to a better product.

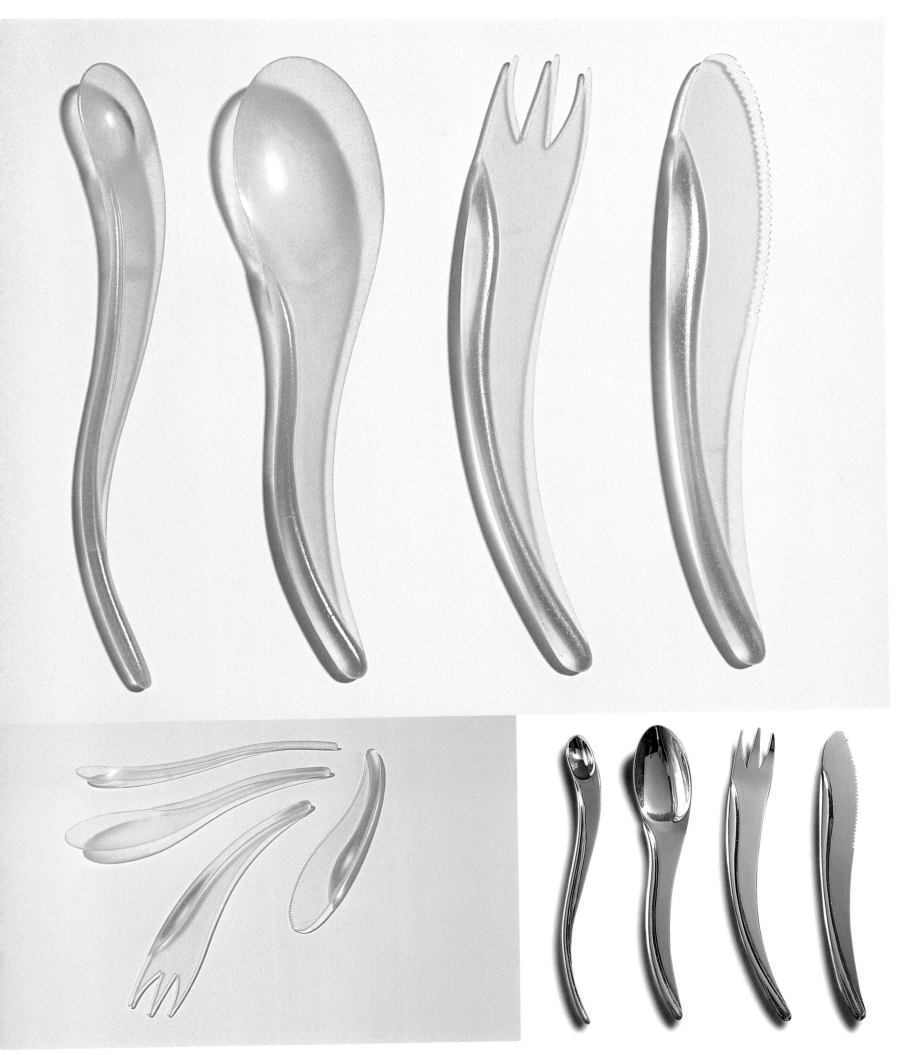

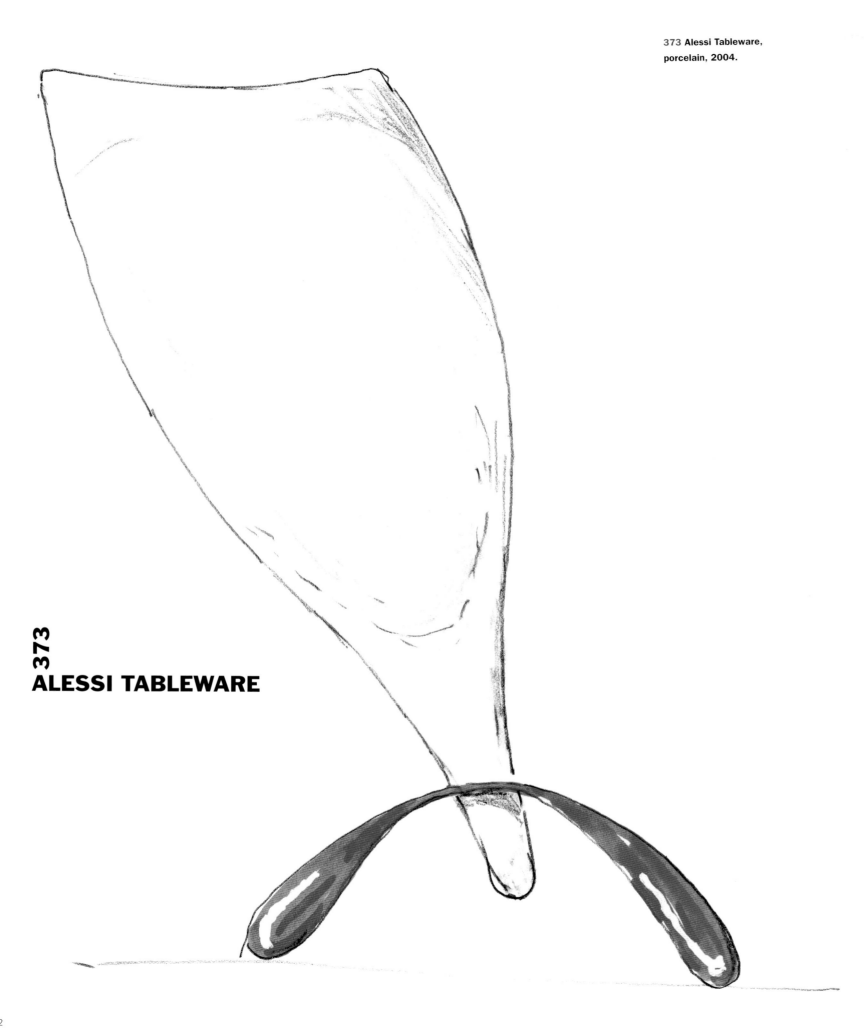

373 Alessi Tableware,
porcelain, 2004.

**373
ALESSI TABLEWARE**

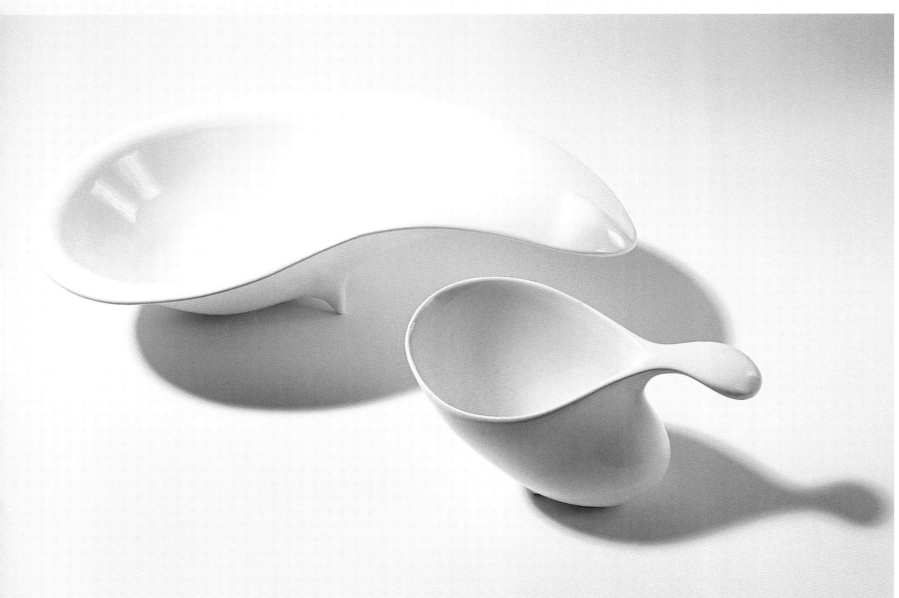

354 Fauteuil, concept project, 2003.

320 Flower Necklace, silver-plated brass, Alessi, 2004.

FLOWER NECKLACE 320

Look at the igloo or the nomadic tent. There is nothing to say that every house has to have eight corners

Jan Kaplicky

Designing a house is the traditional way to start an architectural career. And it is often the measure by which that career is subsequently defined and judged. You could, for example, get a fairly complete picture of the preoccupations of both Le Corbusier and Mies van der Rohe from a close look at the succession of houses that they built at various points in their lives. They are as revealing autobiographically as they are in architectural terms.

Architecture at the domestic scale can be modest enough for a house to be entrusted to an untested, untried architect, but they must still address all the essential elements, social as well as technical. A brief for a house is demanding, detailed and specific, and the architect has to deal with the friction that forms the real point of departure for a design. It can be treated both poetically and pragmatically. A house in this sense can serve not simply as a calling card, but as a kind of manifesto, encapsulating in a surprisingly complete form the wider range of an architect's preoccupations. As such, it is a building type that can be important at every stage in the life of an architectural practice. The house has a significant role to play as a test bed, an experiment with new formal approaches, materials and techniques, and an exploration of alternative ways of living.

Domestic projects have played an important part throughout Future Systems' development. But they have occupied a territory that is rather different from the conventional starting point for an ambitious architectural practice. They have designed two of the more memorable houses to have been built in Britain in the twentieth century, but just as important for Jan Kaplicky is the idea of the house. It has been the inspiration for a series of intense graphic projects that have engaged him since the late 1970s, resulting in a sequence of haunting images. They are speculations not only about the nature of the house, but also the question of how life might be lived, and of the link between the building and the landscape. In these images, Kaplicky has explored our relationship with our possessions, and even the nature of beauty as it is manifested in the creative tension between the mechanical and the organic.

Future Systems have moved back and forth between the perennial practical issues facing every architect who seeks to build within the traditional envelope of the terraced, four-level London house, to speculations about the very nature of the house and domesticity. They have built family homes, holiday houses and apartments. But they have also produced poetic, weightless images of utopian dwellings in natural landscapes free from the constraints of orthogonal geometry and budget, decoupled from the conventional stresses of the architect-client relationship. This is still fertile territory for them. Future Systems' self-initiated designs are not a side issue or a distraction; they are almost as important as the projects in which the practice is engaged in building. It is not only that they point to the directions that subsequent buildings will try to follow, but that they have an inherent validity in themselves.

Some of the most seductive drawings that Kaplicky has produced have been meditations on the technological mutations of the domestic world. The House for a Helicopter Pilot (1979), for example, with its roof-top landing deck, its cushioned lunar-module feet, its built-in solar collectors and its interiors inspired by aircraft cockpits, was delineated with lyrical dream-like precision. It resulted in what looked at first sight like a set of deadpan engineering drawings, but in fact used a far more expressive architectural language. In this project Future Systems were able to play with the idea of impermanence, portability and autonomy in a striking, polemical way that served to update Buckminster Fuller's Dymaxion House (1929). The project implied that the house had been liberated from the dead weight of the earth on which it stood, and that it could move at any moment. The graphic clarity of Kaplicky's pen and ink, juxtaposed with striking photomontaged landscapes, a technique pioneered by Mies van der Rohe, signalled the very detailed nature of the thinking on which the proposal was based. It was designed for real, rather than as a theatrical fantasy.

It was also designed partly as a celebration of the beauty of mechanisms, partly as an exploration of new definitions of domesticity, in which possessions and furniture are integrated with architecture. But it seemed to have learned something from the counter-cultural enthusiasm of the 1970s for self-sufficiency, deploying notional solar energy systems, and even wind power, to sustain life-support bubbles in remote locations. Not far beneath the surface was the imagery of the space programme, which supplied many of the triggers for the

015 **House for a Helicopter Pilot, concept project, 1979.**

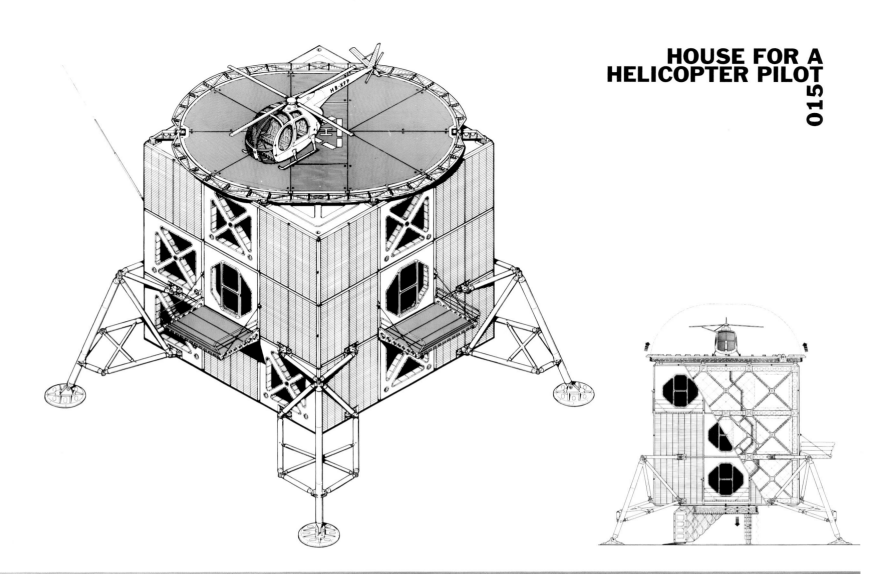

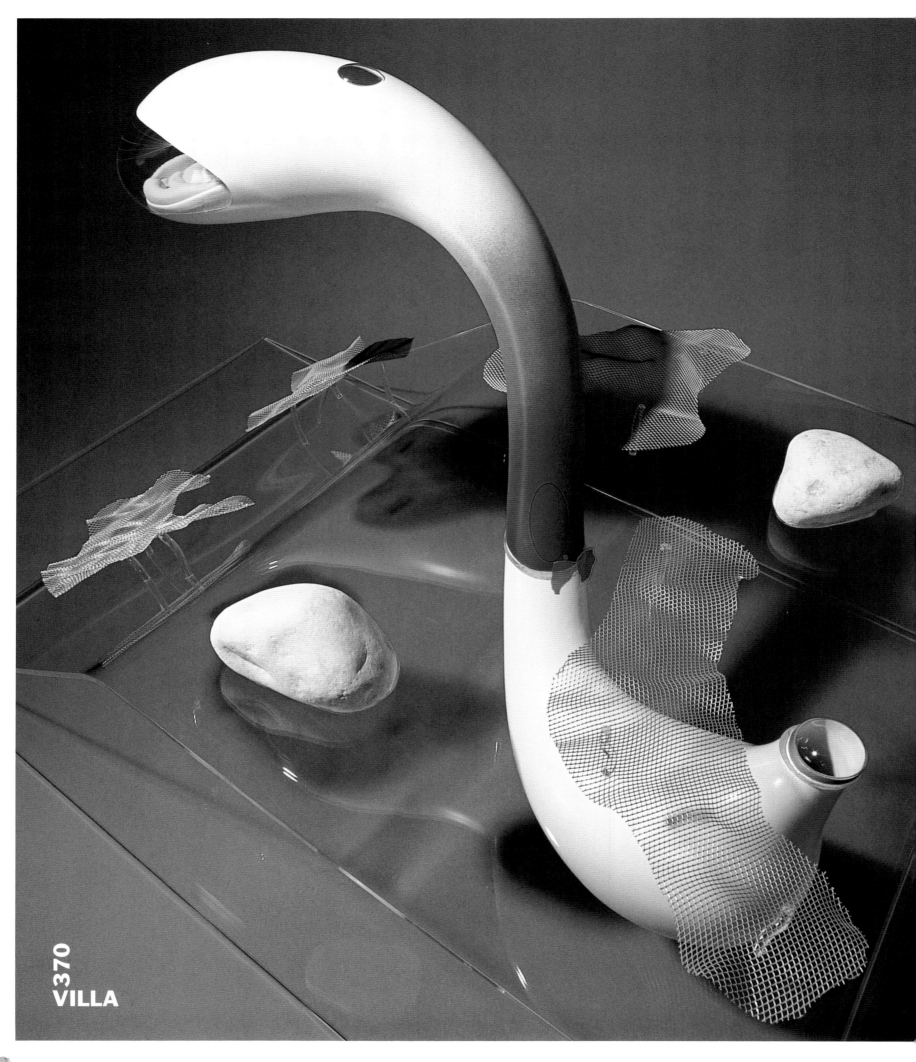

idea of well-serviced life in extreme environments. And for a while in the early 1980s, Future Systems actually did work as consultants to NASA on conceptualizing components for the Space Shuttle programme.

The Helicopter House was a protest against what Kaplicky saw as the dumbness of conventional ideas about what buildings could be, as opposed to the ingenuity and intelligence of mechanisms and machinery. It was an onslaught on the limitations of the brick wall compared to the sheer intelligence of a duraluminum aircraft wing, an attack on the static nature of a solid stone flight of steps, as opposed to the remarkable sight of a flight of steps silently emerging from a slot in the hull of an aircraft at the touch of a hydraulically powered button, and then vanishing again, equally noiselessly. But of course it was also the product of pen and ink, tracing paper and fluorescent tone film, cut by scalpel and applied by hand to the drawing, rather than the effortless fluency of a computer rendering. What distinguished Kaplicky's speculations about autonomous living was the benign view that he took of technology.

While the Green movement rejected technological innovation, for Future Systems it continued to be an inspiration, both as an aesthetic source of ideas, and for speculation about the potential for technology transfer.

Aerospace is the source of a continuing stream of inspirational images and ideas for many architects. The Saturn programme of the early 1960s, with its giant final assembly buildings, was what fired the thinking of the Archigram generation. The Stealth bomber was the origin of a renewed interest in technology, but taking more organic formal directions. And the latest generation of aerospace design has moved on again: combining straight-edged geometry with more fluid forms that intrigue Future Systems.

Even though the early photomontages never became a physical reality; they served to create an aura around Future Systems, and to define the kind of world that they were trying to build. And they still continue to play a significant part in the studio's work.

The Villa project was designed in 2005, after the completion of the Selfridges department store in

370 Villa, concept project, 2005.

Birmingham (1999), where Future Systems fully engaged with the pragmatism and messy reality of the British building industry, and the commercial imperatives of retailing. Designed for one of the wild, idealized landscapes that Kaplicky likes to return to again and again in his work, it has an ethereal quality, and treats the house as a retreat. A remote coastline, apparently untouched by man, an Alpine hideaway, or a desert, have all served as backdrops to decontextualize Kaplicky's designs, and to remove them from the temporal world. The villa could belong to almost any period. It has nothing to do with the 'high-tech' principles that once served to categorize Future Systems' work, and there is perhaps more to connect it with the sculptural explorations that are to be found in the domestic objects on which the practice was working at the time it was designed. The villa is the summation of Kaplicky's speculations about the nature of the domestic environment and his determination to push it into new and ever-more elemental directions.

It takes the form of sinuous monocoque shape, delineated with the glittering hyper-reality of modelling software, though based on a tiny Plasticine working model that Kaplicky twisted and manipulated into shape. The house is in three sections. A tall, swooping form pokes up from the ground, supporting a pod, like a dinosaur's neck and head in a shimmering, complex, curved surface. A second, squatter form protrudes some distance away from the first eruption. Both have Plexiglas visors, smoothly integrated with the skin, to form wrap-around windows. The two are linked by an underground section. A paternoster lift provides access up through the neck to the living area in the taller of the two above-ground sections. A bedroom is formed out of the lower section, with baths and kitchen above ground. The villa is designed to be prefabricated, and installed anywhere, as if it were a private jet, pre-positioned to collect its owners as they zig-zag across the world. The scheme closes a circle that began with the Helicopter House project –

named after the roof-top landing pad that is its most prominent feature – returning to the idea of the house as a fragile bubble, delicately hovering in the landscape.

Kaplicky was designing houses even when he was still a student in Prague. In those days he was under the spell of Frank Lloyd Wright, fascinated by the way in which Wright's architecture achieved an integration between interior and exterior, if not by the master's taste in decorative detail. But a more direct, first-hand inspiration was Adolf Loos. Kaplicky grew up in Prague in a conventional developer's house — for which his father had designed the interiors – which stood just 200 metres away from the Muller House that Loos had built in 1930. 'I remember going to see Mrs Muller with my mother,' he recalls. The House embodied Loos's embrace of the Raumplan idea – the overlapping expression of functional spatial volumes – a concept that clearly left its mark on the young Kaplicky. Later, after the Communist take-over, the house was requisitioned by the party and painted grey, and Kaplicky watched its slow decline.

The first house that Kaplicky designed (1964) was barely completed before he left Czechoslovakia. It could not aspire to the luxurious materials and scale of the Muller House, relying on black-market supplies, and was

328 Ann Swimming Pool, Hertfordshire, 2002.

ANN
SWIMMING
POOL

328

118 **DS Flat, London, 1983.**

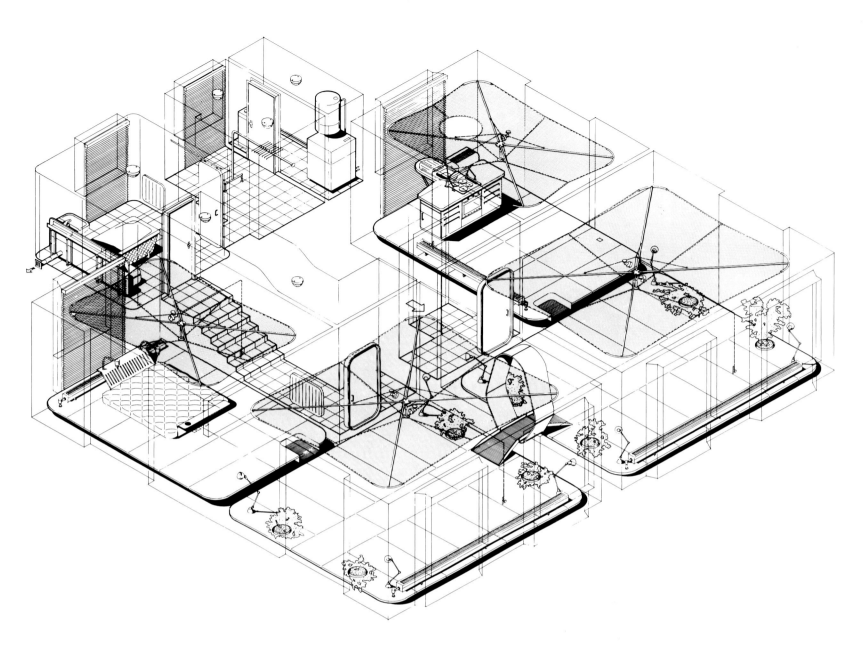

largely self-built by his client, an artist. But modestly scaled though it was, with its painted exposed steel it nevertheless displayed a certain level of ambition. The form was simplicity itself, an 8 metre cube, that could also be understood as a reflection of the cubic volumes of Loos's architecture. It was built by a moonlighting brick-layer, a couple of labourers, who dug the foundations, and the client himself. But the inspiration was, at least in part, Kaplicky's glimpse of America, and the Case Study houses (1940s to 1950s) of Craig Elwood. The studio, where his client painted, was located on the ground floor. The upper level, with the main entrance and with a view of the castle, was where he lived.

Kaplicky completed two more domestic projects in those early days: an attic flat (1958), with a couple of Butterfly chairs copied from a photograph, and a steel ramp (1965). Each of them set out to offer an alternative to the mundane reality of Prague in the early 1960s. 'I was creating a world,' Kaplicky remembers, 'a little self-contained world. Once in it, you were stepping outside Czechoslovakia.'

When Future Systems began to work on domestic

projects in Britain in the 1980s, these had a similar quality, but in London it was the reality of everyday twentieth-century life that you left behind when you stepped inside a Kaplicky door, rather than the Warsaw pact. For three years I lived in an apartment that Future Systems had designed on the second floor of a stucco-fronted nineteenth-century terrace in the swaggering but down-at-heel Victorian suburb of Maida Vale. Every time I negotiated the stone stairs and the cast-iron balustrade to open a front door that looked like an airlock, it felt like I was stepping off the planet into a space craft. Inside was a series of aluminium-floored platforms of varying heights that never came into contact with the walls, connected by more airlocks. Power points, television sockets and lighting fixtures were all integrated into the aluminium. The kitchen appliances were grouped together into a freestanding T-shaped unit. The architects called it a 'culinary workstation', and it had the character of a piece of pared-down equipment borrowed from the flight deck or the operating theatre. One platform came with a bed integrated with the floor. The apartment was a lateral conversion, spreading across the second floor of two adjoining houses, which meant penetrating a load-bearing party wall. Kaplicky devised a main opening that maximized its apparent size without compromising the structure of the house. Its curved parallelogram form seemed to predict the direction he would take in later projects.

Kaplicky had moved to London in 1968 and worked in the office of Denys Lasdun, and subsequently for Piano and Rogers, followed by Norman Foster. His speculations about the nature of the house were his way of putting down a marker for what he would do when he established his own practice. He founded Future Systems in 1979, together with David Nixon, who later moved to America. Rogers bought one of his photomontages, and Peter Cook organized an exhibition of Future Systems' projects at Art Net, the exhibition space that he ran in the late 1970s. This helped to establish the practice as a significant new voice in architecture.

Amanda Levete, who joined Future Systems in 1989 had a different trajectory, closer to the art world, and with less of Kaplicky's view of himself as an outsider. Beginning with a year as an art student and a spell in Will Alsop's office, she launched her architectural career working for YRM, and then spent some years with Richard Rogers. For Levete, architecture did not feel quite so much like an enclave struggling to survive in hostile territory.

After the early projects that Kaplicky built in Prague, when he moved to London his drawings seemed to take on a life of their own for a while. His photomontages and exacting, meticulously delineated axonometrics explored the possibility of using advanced technology to create life-support bubbles in remote locations as vacation retreats or emergency shelter. They pushed the co-option of available components, and the imagery of what was called 'high-tech' at the time, to their ultimate

conclusion. But the point was always to build, and that started to happen in the early 1980s, with series of small projects that served as research exercises, and then to works on a larger scale, a process that gathered momentum when Levete joined the partnership. Her role combined at various times that of critic and organizing force, while developing her own architectural voice within Future Systems.

A series of domestic projects has served to measure out Future Systems' progress from the speculative to the material, through a developing series of aesthetic languages. The first freestanding architectural project that Future Systems realized was a house for the engineer Andy Sedgewick (1990). The next two were major houses, built in the 1990s, which could not be more different in their locations, or their form. The Hauer King House (1992), with its sloping glass facade and spatially complex interior, stands on a nineteenth-century inner London street. The second house, finished five years later, was designed for an independent-minded Labour member of parliament and barrister. It sits on the edge of a Welsh cliff, overlooking the open sea. In the London house, the main ambition was to create a family home within the constraints of a London terrace. The

180 **Hauer King House, London, 1992.**

HAUER KING HOUSE 180

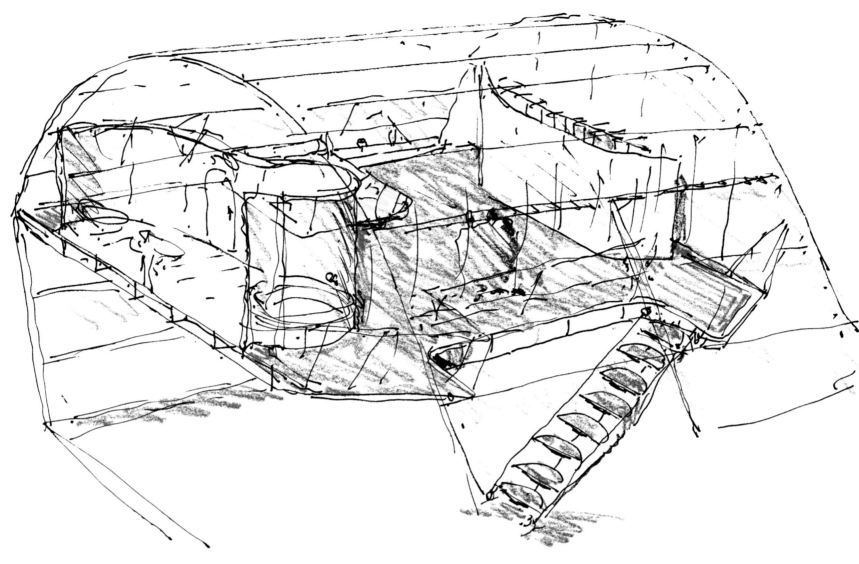

180 Hauer King House,
London, 1992.

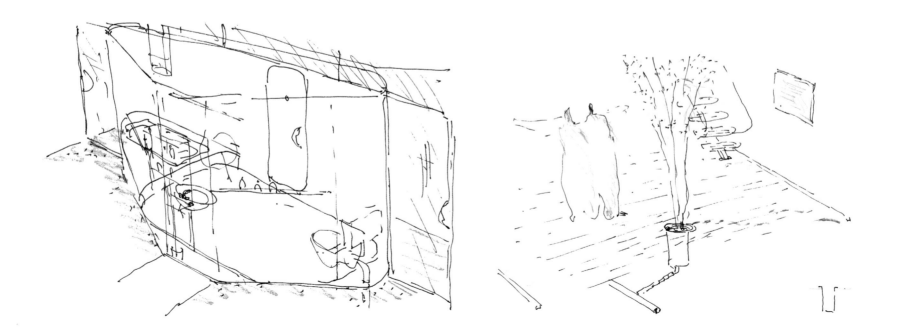

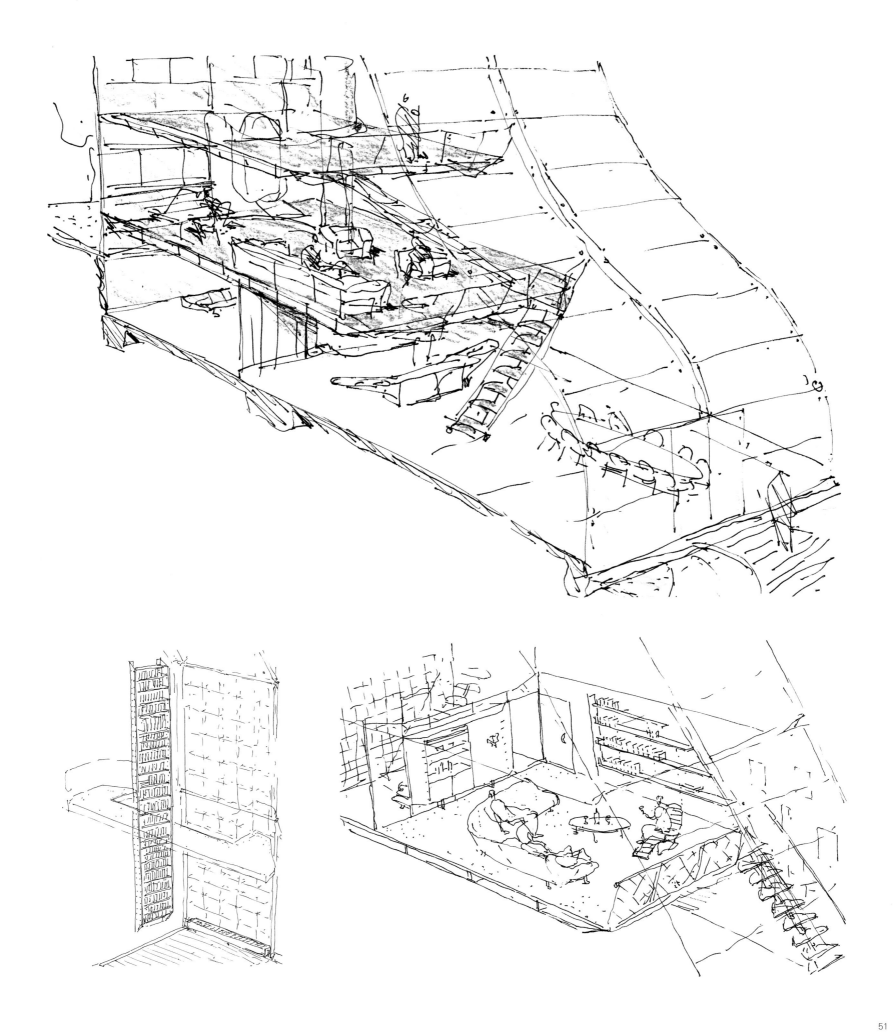

BEDFORD ROW 262

Welsh house took another direction. It reflected a developing interest in softer, more organic forms that could become an integral part of their natural context. All three projects demonstrated that Future Systems was moving beyond the theoretical.

'Designing a house is a journey,' says Levete. 'You have to really like the client. Houses have to be for the right people.' She helped Hauer and King select a site for the new house. They came up with three possibilities, of which the most promising was an end-of-terrace plot in Barnsbury, occupied by a single-storey shed, with planning permission to build a new four-storey house with a facade that replicated that of its Victorian neighbour. 'It was clearly the one,' says Levete. 'I called the planners about the possibility of building a modern house, and they were very encouraging.'

The house managed to introduce a certain spatial excitement through the exploitation of the cross section, with trays of floors that stop short of the facade and introduce a double-height volume. The plan is carefully organized to avoid losing valuable space to fire escapes within a 6-metre-wide plan, where a second staircase would not have worked. The design effort concentrated on the relationship between the kitchen/dining room, on the semi-basement, garden level, and the living room up on the mezzanine that overlooks it, with all the issues this poses for how people actually use a house and its furniture, and the relationship between adults and children. It also attempts to deal with the inherent tendency of the vertically organized terraced house to create dead spaces, with the living area struggling to compete with the kitchen to become the dominant social focus of the house. Says Levete: 'It happens time and again: the raised ground floor ends up being under-used. You hang out in the kitchen. When you have vertical living you have a dead zone, which is never there when it is lateral living. I would always choose a single-level house.'

As the family outgrew the house, they took the decision to move on. Future Systems worked with them on a second occasion in 1998, adding a striking new kitchen to the eighteenth-century terraced house to which they eventually moved. But the first house was widely published, and attracted the attention of the maverick Labour politician Bob Marshall-Andrews and his wife Jill. They called Levete to enquire if Future Systems would be interested in designing a house for a plot of land that they had used for family holidays in Wales.

The resulting house, just 150 metres from the sea, faithfully reflected many of Future Systems' developing enthusiasms. It depended, for example, on prefabrication. Every element used in its construction, including the complete bathroom pods, had to be trucked to the site on a lorry. Its half-concealed nature, surrounded by ramped earth, and with a turf roof whose elliptical glass windscreen emerged from the grass, was a form that developed from a series of Future Systems' competition designs for much larger-scale projects, beginning with their submission for the first Parthenon Museum competition (1990). But it was also rooted in the specifics of place and the personality of the clients. The house had to be as unobtrusive as possible, without losing the all-important view. It was an area of considerable natural beauty, where planning permission for a new house was only available because of an existing structure, a barrack-like hut on the site. It was completed in 1997, by which time the organic shapes that excited Future Systems were becoming more achievable. 'When the Hauer King House was done, you couldn't do curved glass at an affordable price,' said Future Systems. 'That has changed.'

Digging into the ground would have lowered the house's profile, but would also have lost the view of the sea from the interior. Instead, Future Systems used ramped earth and turf on the roof to make the house inconspicuous, but kept the floor level up, and built in a 300 mm high platform in the main living space that gives an eye-level view out over the sea. The house is just 150 m², but feels more spacious, in part because of the direct relationship with the view, but also because of the way in which the architects have incorporated seating and furniture within the architectural shell. While maximizing the sense of the spectacular in the main living space, the plan carefully separates the main bedroom from the two guest bedrooms located on the other side of the house. In the rural setting, Future Systems wanted to avoid self-consciously artful materials and details. Kaplicky uses the word 'innocent' as the objective. The glass wall is ventilated by circular portholes bought from a yachting-supplies store. The roof is highly insulated plywood. The drainage system depends on a septic tank.

The ideal domestic environment for Future Systems is one in which structure and content blur seamlessly into one, so that floors can be both soft and hard, act as circulation space as well as seating, storage as well as structure. Architecture is envisaged as an integrated, intelligent system that responds to human needs, dealing with climate-control and context as required, rather than being monumental or formal.

For Future Systems, it should be possible to find enough light to read a book by anywhere in a house, rather than only within the constraints of the single beam of a fixed reading light. According to this view, the idea of a sofa seems like the memory of an old-fashioned approach to the interior, no matter how it is designed, or what materials it uses. The most truly modern approach for Future Systems is to abolish the seat as a discreet element altogether, and to replace it with a soft floor that could shape itself around the occupants as they wanted, rising and falling to take full advantage of a view, or provide a more comfortable seating position.

With each new housing project, Future Systems seek to challenge preconceived views about what constitutes a home. 'Somewhere in all Westerners, there is a trace of Greek classical thinking, but other cultures don't have that,' says Kaplicky. 'Look at the igloo or the nomadic tent. There is nothing to say that every house has to have eight corners.' For Future Systems, the advantage of a more organic geometry is the freedom that it brings:

It allows you to introduce height in the right places. You don't need a seven metre overall height, when you can go up or down where it's needed; it means more drama, but also more functionality. It's possible to start to experiment with floor levels, perhaps with semi-curved floors; you don't have to have a wall – maybe it disappears altogether. It is a theory, but things are moving in that direction.

Sit 30 cm above the floor, and you have a totally different feel, it makes you sit just a little higher, but it totally changes how you see the house. The relationship between standing and sitting is critical. Frank Lloyd Wright was short, so he made bedrooms that were just 193 cm high. He liked to build caves. It's like a theatre: you build new floors. Do you adjust it, or does it adjust to you? Is the house a mechanism? I don't like to use 'flexibility' – it's misused, it's degraded as a word. What we want is flexibility to be spontaneous, we don't want it to be mechanical.

262 Bedford Row, extension, London, 1998.

222 House in Wales,
Pembrokeshire, 1994.

222 **House in Wales,**
Pembrokeshire, 1994.

The themes explored by Future Systems' earlier rural houses are taken a step further by their plans for a new house on a Kent farm drawn up in 2005. The teardrop-shaped single-storey house is designed to make its occupants as much a part of the landscape as possible, while minimizing its own visual impact. The house is an attempt at a practical realisation of Kaplicky's speculative designs for autonomous dwellings with the lightest of footprints. There is no visible roadway, just a reinforced grass track leading to an integral parking place within the envelope of the house. Internally, the spaces are differentiated from each other but still connected visually.

What a single family house cannot do is to explore the ways in which people can live together in cities, an issue that has interested Kaplicky since his first sight of Zlin, the industrial suburb built in the 1930s by the Bata shoe company. At a research level, it has inspired Future Systems' explorations of the high-rise as a residential building type, as well as their attempts to integrate wind generators within high-rise urban housing. This concept constitutes the next step for the practice, with a project for an apartment block in Denmark commissioned in 2004, and studies for an apartment tower in Manhattan.

389 Copenhagen, apartment building, 2004.

COPENHAGEN **389**

406 House Kent, 2005.

SHO

We don't want to be fashionable architects, but we are interested in the idea of fashion

Jan Kaplicky

255 **Comme des Garçons New York, fashion store, 1998.**

Despite an approach to questions of ornament that might be described as verging on the stern, Adolf Loos was actually fascinated by the issue of fashion. There are animated essays among his collected writings about precisely what it was that made Germans wear their trousers too wide, and the way in which turn-of-the-century hat-makers used to conspire together to determine what would constitute fashion for the next season. His interest in the subject went well beyond mere intellectual curiosity. Loos was responsible for what is probably the first example of an architect-designed fashion shop, a reminder to those who still see fashion and retail design as essentially frivolous commissions for an architect that such projects can also offer substance. In fact, Loos produced at least three designs for retail-fashion outlets that were far from being merely machines for selling things. Goldman Salatsch's premises (1910–11), at the back door of the Imperial Palace in Vienna, are now used as a bank and an exhibition space. A couple of streets away, Knize, the gentlemen's outfitters from whose Berlin branch Mies van der Rohe once ordered his immaculately tailored suits and his silk handkerchiefs, was also built by Loos in 1910. With its elegantly refined brass and mahogany cabinets, and its glass vitrines, it is still in business, even

if the merchandise isn't quite what it was. As it happens, Knize's Prague branch was designed by Loos as well. It did not manage to survive four decades of Communism, but it lasted long enough to leave a profound impression on the young Kaplicky. He knew all about Loos's complex mix of profoundly radical intentions, sensuous materials and luxurious restraint, and he found it a highly seductive proposition. As a student, he even had a copy of Loos's essays.

By the time Kaplicky moved to London, he had already decided that fashion was not something for an architect to be afraid of, despite the long and uneasy relationship between the two disciplines. And he found other architectural inspirations for retail design. He cites the shop that Wells Coates designed for Cresta (1929), as well as the elegance of the Simpsons and Heals stores in London, as setting architectural precedents for the well-crafted polish of the Future Systems approach to retail design.

In spite of the feverish experimentation of the 1960s, and the overwhelming impact on London of the pop-culture wave, the England of 1967 still believed deep down that serious architecture was meant to last for a long time, and that real architects did not get involved with something as transient as fashion or shopping. It was not a conviction that touched Kaplicky, who did not feel much sense of connection with the architectural community that took this jaundiced view. His unabashed fascination with innovation went beyond the traditional definitions of architecture. And his passionate enthusiasm for striking imagery of all kinds served to inoculate him from any such prejudice. Three decades later, he could still point to a photograph of a Paco Rabanne-designed metal-disc dress from the 1960s as an inspiration for the curvaceous skin of Selfridges department store in Birmingham. He also took an excited interest in the way that fashion could experiment with new technologies in materials. But this was not about the neophyte pursuit of novelty for its own sake. For Kaplicky, the attraction of fashion was partly to be found in the contrast it made with the resolutely conformist nature of the Warsaw-pact style that he had endured for so many years in Prague. During his years spent on the wrong side of the Iron Curtain, where he had grown his hair dangerously long and adopted the even more risky style of authentic US army surplus jackets, he had absorbed from a distance the West's freedom to experiment. It was this comparison between tedium and excitement that made the glossy surface sheen of fashion look particularly appealing.

In those early days in London, Carnaby Street and the exotic shops that lined it seemed like an explosion of all the things that Prague could only dream of. As he commuted to his job in Denys Lasdun's office, Kaplicky's bus took him along the King's Road every day. Its route went directly past the Chelsea Drug Store, designed by Garnett Cloughley Blakemore in 1964, with its shiny chrome and steel facade, and its pop graphics. Long forgotten now, for a brief moment it was the most fashionable store on the most fashionable street in the world. In its present-day incarnation it is the most convenient branch of McDonalds for the old soldier

341 New Look, fashion store, London, 2002.

pensioners of the Royal Hospital, a reminder of the abbreviated life span of the average retail interior. 'You were aware of a new shop opening every second day,' Kaplicky recalls wistfully of the London of those days, and, indeed, he briefly worked for Garnett Cloughley Blakemore himself. 'Fashion and architecture have a very strange relationship,' he says. 'People sometimes ask us, "Why are you doing it?" But shapes and colours are very important for us. We don't want to be fashionable architects, but we are interested in the idea of fashion.'

What underpins Future Systems' view of fashion is a kind of confrontation between the ideas that created Adolf Loos's Knize, and the pursuit of the new as represented by the Chelsea Drug Store, albeit translated into the very different climate of the new century, with its rapidly developing possibilities for working with new geometries and pushing materials in new directions. That period has its echo in Future Systems' recent work for New Look's Oxford Street store (2002), with its mirror-finished, polished-metal stairs, which look like a cascade of liquid mercury, and its sharply acidic colour schemes. Unlike their earlier work for Commes des Garçons and Marni, New Look is very much at the budget end of the market. 'Part of the appeal was to do a place that was for everybody,' says Levete. 'When we went to New Look's headquarters, we were fascinated by the energy they bring to what they do. Everything is done with so much speed; they respond very quickly to the market, and they can deliver clothes to their stores two or three times a day.' And Levete, who retains an anarchic streak, clearly took a certain relish in overturning preconceptions that architecture was only applicable as the glossy couture end of retailing.

Early on in its life, Future Systems worked closely with Eva Jiricna on the design of Way In, the boutique fashion floor of Harrods that was comprehensively remodelled at the start of the 1980s in an attempt to inject some youthful credibility into what was then the sleeping giant of the department-store world. It was one of the studio's first realized projects, and a chance to put all its speculation about materials and mobility into practice. The design took the form of a kit of parts: display units on wheels that could be redeployed on the Way In floor as required, and demountable screens to define Way In territory. But it wasn't until much later that Future Systems became regularly involved with shops in general and fashion in particular, by which time Levete had joined the practice and brought her own sensibilities and perspectives to the partnership. Levete's fashion sense came from her time as an art student in London, and later at the Architectural Association, where she discovered the thrift shops and the vintage clothes that twenty years later were to inspire Marni's approach to fashion. 'I enjoy fashion, especially British fashion, which so often comes from the street, from really young people, and then is made more sophisticated,' she says.

In part it is the sense of creative freedom accom–panying the idea of fashion that appeals to Kaplicky and Levete. Working with fashion is a chance to see quick results, and to search for fresh ideas. And partly it is the energy and the imagination that fashion demands of an architect that makes it so hard to turn down the chance to design a store for a creative fashion designer. Kaplicky sees the inventiveness and creativity that goes into a fashion collection as comparable to the constant search for performance-boosting innovation that goes into the design of a Formula One car. But fashion also involves architecture, with an audience that is much wider than the narrowly defined architectural community. It gives architecture the chance to be popular.

Two things happen at once in the process of designing a fashion store. Firstly, the architect is asked to create a complete emotional world for a specific designer's clothes, an environment that encapsulates the mood that the designer is trying to project, in the way that the artwork for an album cover used to do, or more prosaically, like a corporate identity programme for an airline. When a fashion brand is considering a world-wide approach, including freestanding stores as well as franchises in shopping outlets, diffusion labels and accessories and perfumes, the process of designing a shop is even more closely linked to the business-like projection of identity. And at the same time, there is the rigorous technical task of putting the clothes on show and making them look as desirable as possible. That is a question that touches on exactly how the clothes are displayed, and how much of the stock is actually on show at any one time. Cramming in as much as possible on the sales floor is a strategy that is economical with space, and helps shoppers find a garment quickly, but it does not make the most of each individual item, which benefits from being given as much space to itself as is

341
NEW LOOK

practical. The shop is there to attract and entice, to make the clothes look their best, and to make the customers look good too, when they try them on.

Clothes can be understood as the cast in a theatrical production, placed in the stage set of the shop that the architect has built. The shop window is a poster, and an advertisement for the production inside. But there is always the sense of avoiding the obvious, the literal and the lifelike. Hanging clothes in a eye-catching way, using lighting to make the most of colour and texture, and suggesting combinations, is more effective. Giving the shop an attractive external presence also relies on subtle treatment of the window display. The strategy of simply filling the window with obvious lures has become so predictable that not only elite fashion but the fashion mainstream is several steps beyond it now. The shop window acts as a kind of filter, signalling what lies within, and even adopting a challenging aesthetic that warns those who are uncomfortable with what they see that they will be unlikely to enjoy the clothes on offer inside. Twenty years ago, elite fashion decided that the most effective come-on for its customers was to play hard to get. If the door wasn't actually locked, then the window

display might be entirely empty. In this irony-abundant world, we are probably ready for another bout of the counter-intuitive, wide-open shop window by now. Irony or not, there is always the need to allow customers to try on the clothes comfortably.

Such are the complexities of fashion branding that it is no longer enough to rely on any single architect or look, or to use the signature of a prominent architect as a kind of endorsement. A decade ago, fashion brands created shops that were ruthlessly identical in every city, suggesting that fashion was a kind of cult, and every item with the right label that came from the store, whether it was bought in Aoyama or Bond Street, carried the same essential aura. It was a uniformity that betrayed more social anxiety than confidence. As a response to that realization, flagship stores are now routinely designed to be different around the world. Even within a single store, various designers can be responsible for distinct elements.

The first such commission for Future Systems came in 1998 from Rei Kawakubo, the Japanese designer behind the Commes des Garçons label, for a series of designs for individual stores in Tokyo, New York and

341 New Look, fashion store, London, 2002.

Paris. For the Harrods project, so many years before, Future Systems' role had been closer to industrial design than architecture, and involved the design of a range of mobile fittings. Working with Commes des Garçons gave Future Systems the chance to create a series of large-scale sculptural objects in a range of materials, operating in quite different ways in each store, which themselves had different customers and different product ranges.

In the years since the completion of Way In, with its all-black walls and floors, architecture has become an essential part of most fashion brands' repertoire. Each of the major fashion names has formed an association with a more or less high-profile architect. The idea was partly to create the association of exclusivity that a major architect can bring, partly to create a sense of aura around the store, and partly to look as distinctively different from the other major figures participating in the struggle for media attention as possible. Ironically it was the very sense of permanence that architecture could bring that seemed to count most.

Architects with something to offer fashion had become sought after by this time, and Future Systems' introduction to Rei Kawakubo was made by Ronnie

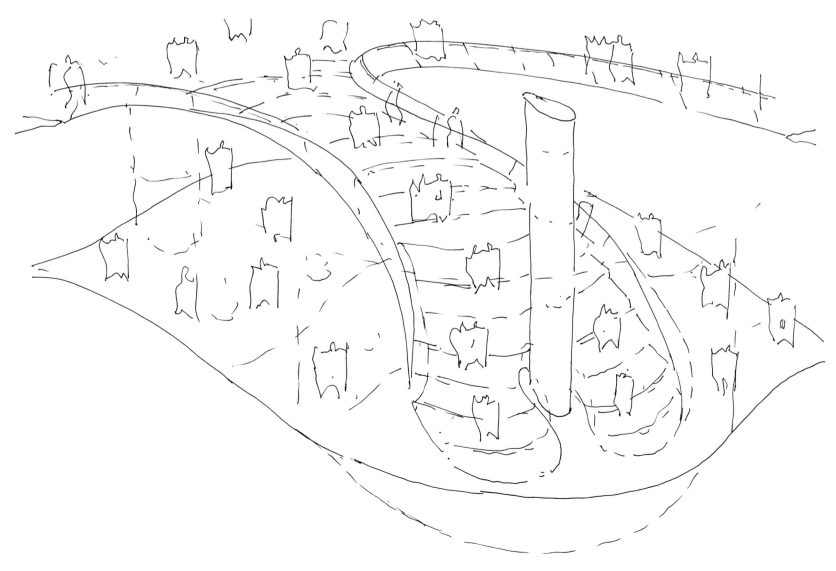

257 Comme des Garçons
Toyko, fashion store, 1998.

You can't say 'found' space is non-space. It sounds artless, but actually it is very carefully chosen **Amanda Levete**

Newhouse, a consultant specializing in the issue of image for fashion companies. She was married to Jonathan Newhouse, European chairman of the Condé Nast empire, for whom Future Systems were later to design an office. Despite the Way In project, when they met Kawakubo, Future Systems were categorized as having had no previous retail experience. But this apparent limitation was in fact a positive advantage. Future Systems had no instantly recognizable signature to bring to fashion interiors. Nor were they over-identified with any one fashion name – an association that could create a confused image in terms of branding. However, Kawakubo did not really want them to design a complete shop for her. As a designer who has continually attempted to bring a fresh, new language to everything she does, this was a moment in her career when she was looking for another new direction for her stores. In her early days she had worked with raw concrete and sparse, almost empty interiors, long before this had become an overworked shorthand for Japanese fashion. But the introduction of shadow gaps between wall and floor, and Portuguese limestone floors, the next universal fashion look, was not for Kawakubo; it was simply too ubiquitous a language. The creation of a gallery-like atmosphere for shirts and jackets was ready-made and predigested, an obvious way to equate fashion with art. Commes des Garçons wanted something else. 'When she came to see us in London,' says Kaplicky:

I really thought that she wouldn't give the job to us. But Kawakubo was free enough in her thinking to go for a firm with no real shop experience. Her only stipulation was that the store would last for ten years. It wasn't about designing a shop; it was a kind of artistic collaboration. We wouldn't have done just a facade for any other client. The shop for us wasn't a functional issue. We didn't have to worry about managing clothes; we never talked about how you get people in. It was cerebral. Kawakubo doesn't like having a single hand doing the whole thing. It's an aesthetic for her: in her shop, she sells her own line, and other people's as well.

Kawakubo allowed Future Systems to be themselves, to make a creative response to the particular space they were working with, similar to the way in which she had collaborated with a succession of artists over the years to make installations in her shops. Kawakubo has always been far too smart for a single house style. Her brand image is to be constantly on the look-out for new and interesting work of all kinds, without any stylistic preconceptions about what that might be.

Future Systems' subsequent fashion interiors depend on an understanding of what is really happening in the shop, and what it needs to do to work effectively. That is partly a question of enticement, partly of making the products themselves look as good as possible, but it is also the creation of a distinct atmosphere that makes the shop recognizable for what it is. The fashion store is perhaps the most extreme and developed form of shop, pushed to its ultimate expression in a hot-house

**260 Comme des Garçons
Paris, fashion store, 1998.**

environment of continuous development, driven by competition and the constant hunger for novelty. The three stores on which Future Systems worked for Commes des Garçons are all different from each other. They have varying contexts, and the degree of Future Systems' involvement also varied. They were working less as shop designers than as part of a group of designers, architects and artists, each making a contribution to the overall nature of the store.

For Kawakubo's Tokyo flagship on Omotesando, Japan's Bond Street, on a stretch of the most concentrated crush of high-profile retail design in the world, they made what was probably the first use of three-dimensionally curved glass in Japan to create an undulating wave that swoops in and out between the structural columns that support the uneventful, generic Tokyo commercial building of which Commes des Garçons forms the ground floor. 'The idea of a wavy glass wall … meant a ten or fifteen per cent reduction in floor space, but Kawakubo accepted it,' says Levete. Retail space in one of Tokyo's most expensive streets is the greatest luxury of all, and to dispose of it so generously is the clearest signal of contemporary luxury. The ribbon of glass is 50 metres long, and was made in Spain. Achieving the curves was a considerable technical achievement and, in recognition of Tokyo's vulnerability to earthquakes, required the addition of steel stiffeners in as unobtrusive a way as possible. 'We thought that colour was very important too. We used blue, because there is simply nothing else like it in the area,' says Kaplicky.

In New York, Kawakubo opened a store in an area that could not be more different from Omotesando. The stretch of West 22nd Street chosen for the Commes des Garçons store housed nothing more than Max Protech's art gallery, aside from the industrial lofts, the engineering workshops and the surviving outposts of the meat market. That was the main attraction for Kawakubo, who was trying to suggest that she was not confined to the conventional parameters of fashion, a suggestion that is of course a flattering one for her customers. For this store, carved out of Heavenly Bodies, an old car-repair shop, the major requirement was that nothing of the design could be seen on the brick street facade. Despite the rapid pace of gentrification, the area was still not a place in which to offer ram-raiders too tempting a target. At night the whole store is invisible behind its shutters. But the low-key exterior also treats the neighbourhood with respect, and avoids creating the impression that the shop is a piece of militant imperialism by the fashion world, colonizing and transforming yet another part of the city. The choice of this 'found space' for the shop is very close to the enthusiasm of cutting-edge art galleries for recycling industrial lofts. But, as Levete says, 'you can't just find any space. Found space, may sound artless, but actually it's just as "artful" as being artful about designing it. You can't say its a non-space.'

Future Systems were asked to demonstrate that this was a new kind of environment, and to establish a slight sense of mystery and other-worldliness. Their work deliberately plays off the raw brickwork of the old building

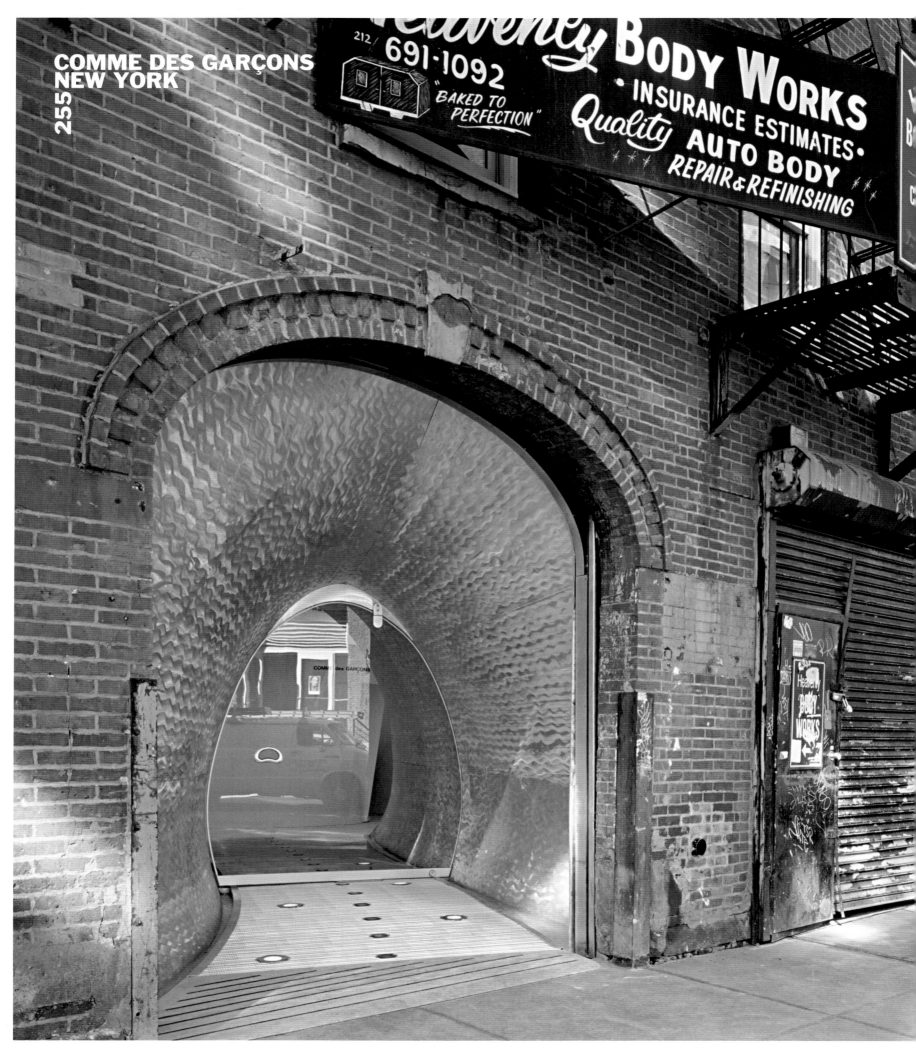

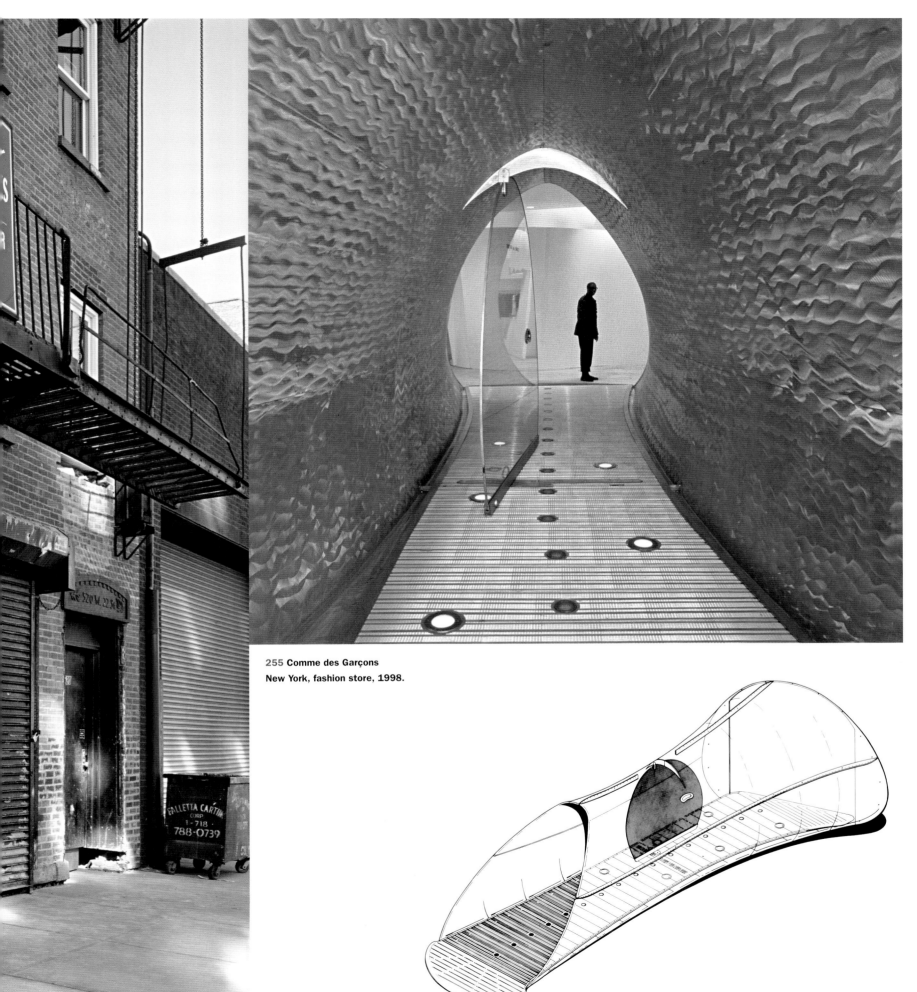

255 Comme des Garçons
New York, fashion store, 1998.

255 Comme des Garçons New York, fashion store, 1998.

273 Marni London,
fashion store, 1999.

that has been left battered and untouched on the street front, complete with the original painted sign. One proposal had the tongue profile of their steel ramp protruding in elevation, but this was too much of a statement for Kawakubo. In the end they designed a steel tunnel that feels like a drawbridge, encouraging you to penetrate the somewhat hostile street front. But once the revised version was approved, fabrication went ahead without a hitch. 'In one afternoon,' say Future Systems, 'we sat with the boat builder who would make it and an engineer. We decided that we could do it with 6 mm aluminium plate, like the Media Centre at Lords.' The five pieces were fabricated by the specialist boat builder in Cornwall, the same contractor who had worked on the Media Centre, and were transported to New York in standard shipping containers. The aluminium plate is finished in an entirely different way from the London project, with tightly abraded circular marks. The inspiration was the engine blocks of the supremely elegant Bugatti sports car.

The third Future Systems project for Commes des Garçons was for a small shop in the Place Vendôme, in Paris, which is different again, an interior slipped into a carefully protected historic environment to create a perfume boutique. 'Colour is what has most effect in the situation. We chose red, because it's very unusual; red has no relationship with this location, just as in Tokyo we chose blue as the dominant colour because it's totally different from anything down the road,' says Kaplicky. Levete calls the Paris design 'a simple veil'. The intense pink at the base of the facade fades to clear at the top. But it was still very hard to get it past the French planning system. 'We argued that you could take it away and leave no marks.'

When Marni came to see Future Systems, they had a very different problem from Commes des Garçons, which already had a high profile and was looking to demonstrate its continuing energy and commitment to innovation. The family-owned Milanese company had started out two generations previously in the fur

273 **Marni London, fashion store, 1999.**

298 **Marni Paris,**
fashion store, 2001.

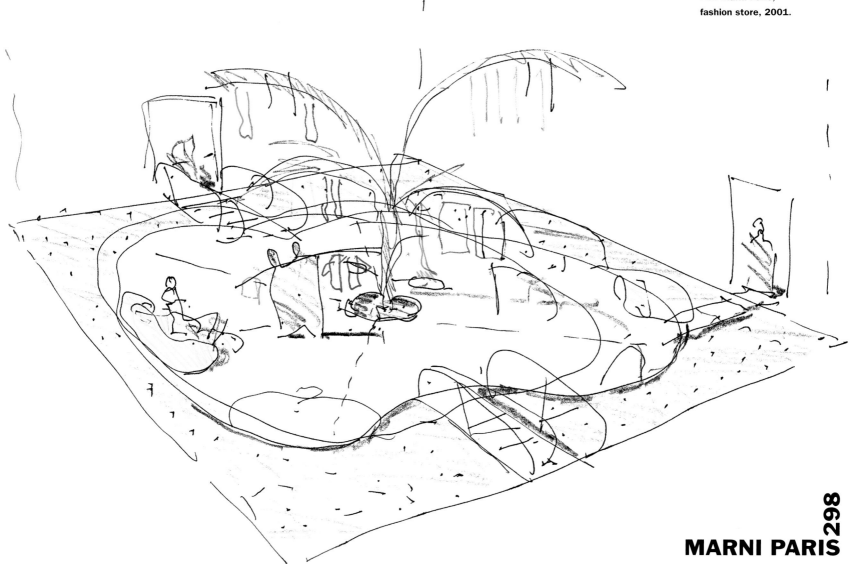

MARNI PARIS 298

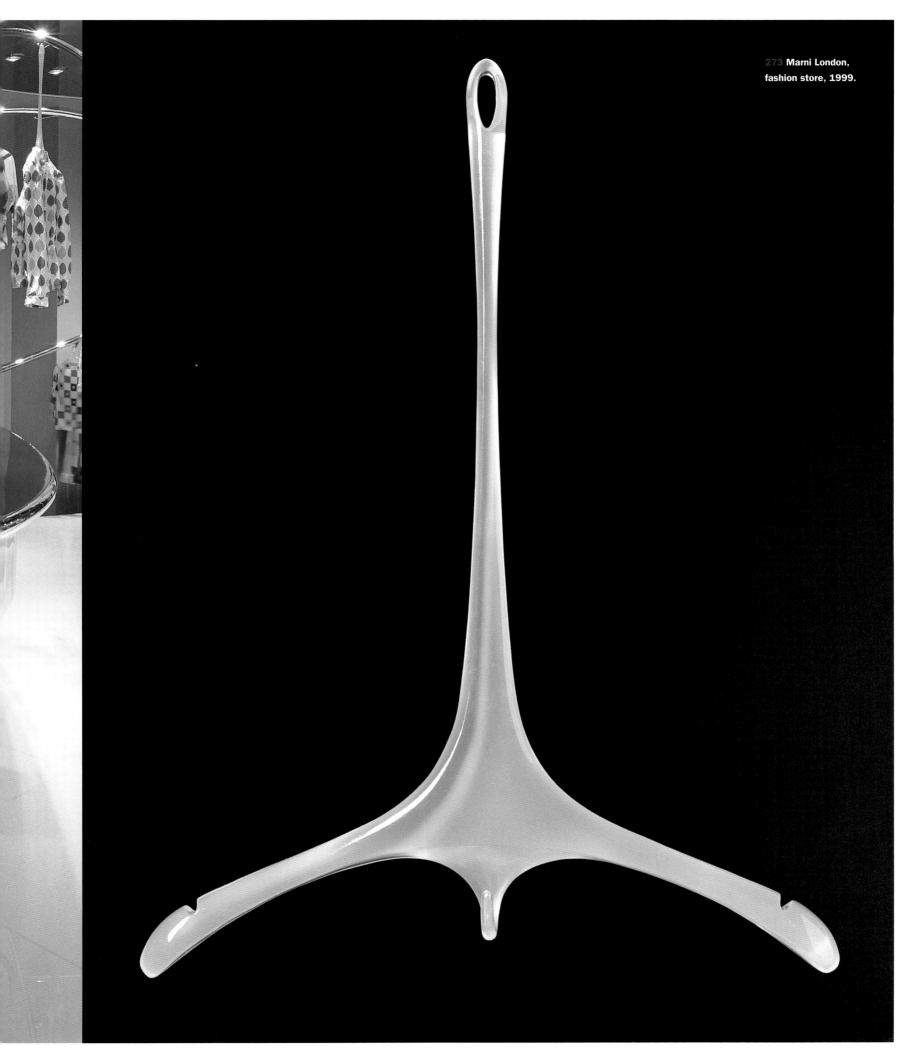

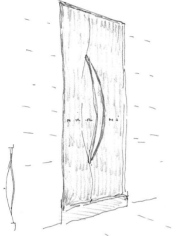

273 Marni Milan,
fashion store, 1999.

business, then moved into fashion through mail order, and by the beginning of 1999 was looking to establish a retail presence in Britain, where it had no brand recognition. Marni asked Future Systems for a look that would make them stand out in the crowded, image-conscious fashion streets – from Sloane Street in London to the via Montenapoleone in Milan – that are the essential locations for every new brand trying to establish its credibility. Future Systems initially designed a store in London that was to guide the look for new shops in Milan, Paris and New York.

The strategy here was to use a different colour in a powerful, very direct way in each store, to give it a distinctive look that responded to its setting in a manner that let it stand out. Future Systems concentrated their energy on a few basic items, transforming what might have been mundane into a distinctive language for the shops. They wanted to give Marni stores a beautiful floor, an area that they believed was an afterthought in most fashion interiors. They used reconstituted glass, which can be given a mirror finish but is reasonably economical and sets off the polished stainless-steel fittings that unite display racks and counters in a single, swooping overall composition. Three variations of specially made Perspex hangers that look as if they have liquefied and are melting off the racks turn the clothes into the real stars of the interior by presenting them in profile.

309 Selfridges Food Hall, Manchester, 2001.

SELFRIDGES CHILDREN'S DEPARTMENT

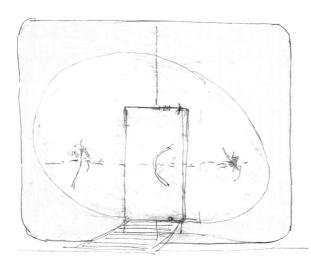

In the Milan store, the window and the door are subtly distorted, like distended soap bubbles in glass and steel, communicating with maximum effect in the most minimal space the nature of the shop inside. This involved applying heat at various points to the glass. It was done on a gas burner, with more heat applied in some places than others so that it sagged at the required points. Then a pattern of fritted dots was applied to the interior surface.

Without turning into shop-fitters, or themselves being consumed by fashion – always a danger for architects – Future Systems have been able to use this series of fashion commissions aimed at audiences as diverse as the teenagers who spend Saturdays in New Look, and the affluent and well-travelled customers of Commes des Garçons, to explore the possibilities of materials and geometry. Even more importantly, they have employed them as a way of creating distinctive environments, each of which seems to offer a glimpse of another world that remains just over the horizon, the target that Future Systems have always pursued. Beyond the fashion interiors that they have done, which include the children's department in the Oxford Street Selfridges, and the food halls in its Manchester and Birmingham stores, there has been a succession of shop spaces on larger and smaller scales. But there is no single Future Systems approach to designing a shop. Sometimes they work on an architectural scale, using space and height, as at the food halls, at other times, and with equal confidence, they operate on a miniature scale. Wild at Heart, for example, is a kind of jewel case for exotic plant species. 'A shop like that is a place where you can't cheat. It's a place where every mistake you make is visible. It means getting the little details just right,' say the designers.

For Future Systems, designing a shop is a matter of creating a seductive environment that offers visitors something they cannot get elsewhere, which explains why they tend to avoid an over-reliance on screens or electronics in their work. They see shopping as a form of refuge from the everyday world, a highly theatrical landscape for what is essentially a playful activity. 'People watch television at home every day so why show it to them in the shop as well?' asks Kaplicky. 'Shopping is a human activity, you can't, or at least, you shouldn't, make it mechanical.'

249 Wild at Heart, flower shop, London, 1997.

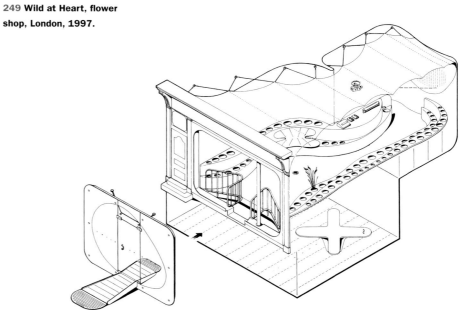

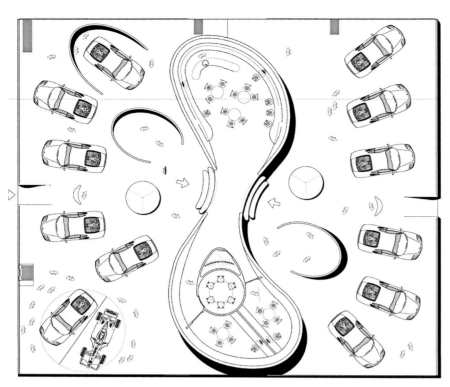

333 Ferrari Maserati,
exhibition stand, Paris, 2002.

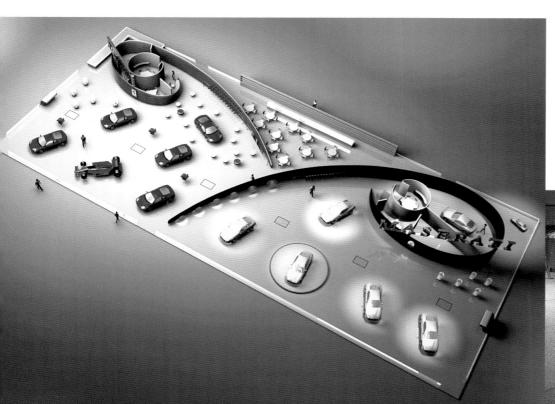

316 Ferrari Frankfurt,
exhibition stand, 2001.

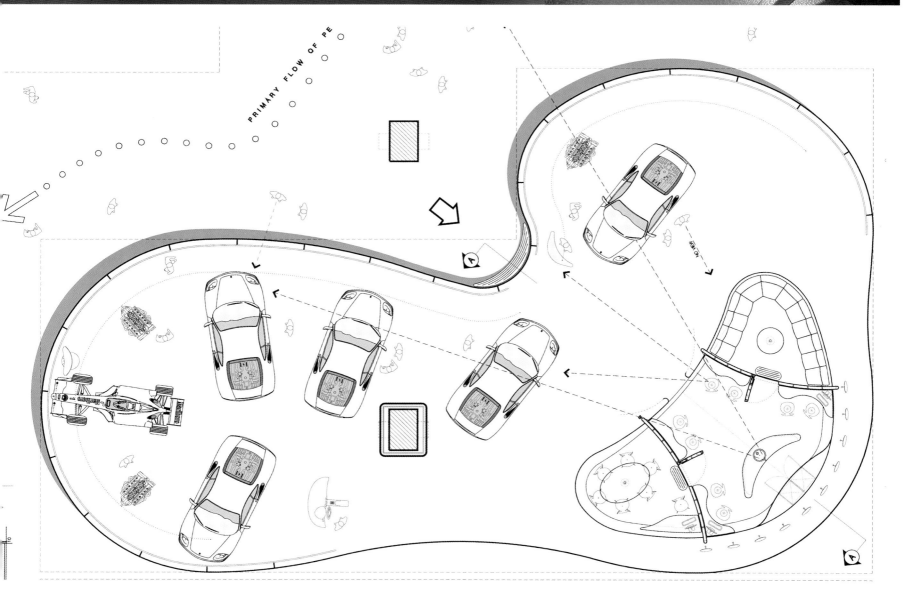

COL
ORAT

Architects are used to working as part of a team. For them, an artist is another person on the team. Artists are used to working with a singular vision

Amanda Levete

351 Naples Subway, Monte Sant'Angelo Station, 2003.

EGG CINEMA

342

Just after World War II, when the French Catholic Church invited an elderly Henri Matisse to decorate a new chapel for a convent in Vence in the hills above Nice, it was suggested to him that he might want to collaborate on the project with an architect. According to Hilary Spurling, Matisse's biographer, the name of Le Corbusier was mentioned as a suitable candidate. Matisse hastily declined the suggestion, and instead turned for architectural advice to an old acquaintance, the rather more biddable Auguste Perret.

Matisse's painted ceramic tiles *Stations of the Cross* filling most of one wall, his three stained-glass windows, and his design for the confessional door screen are among the greatest examples of twentieth-century religious art, representing a remarkably bold, even unsettling creative breakthrough. The chapel itself, however, is little more than banal as a piece of architecture. It is barely competent, let alone a stylistic landmark, and the gulf between the ambition of the art and the pragmatism of the architecture betrays the curious lack of sympathy or even interest in an architectural vision displayed by many artists.

Would an architectural context as distinguished in its own way as Matisse's art have made more of it? Or would it have upstaged or diminished it, as the artist so clearly feared it would? The idea of collaboration between artists and architects, supposedly so desirable in the abstract, has rarely been a straightforward process. In theory, it is universally accepted that art cannot be used as a cosmetic afterthought to camouflage architectural shortcomings, and that effective collaboration depends on the involvement of the artist at the very beginning of the design process. In other words, a partnership in which each side impacts on the work of the other. But that theory hardly reflects the conflicted nature of creativity. Generosity of spirit is not necessarily an aspect of the psychological make-up of even the most talented artist or architect.

More often, collaborative projects begin with the best possible intentions, and end badly. While Richard Serra, for example, may have worked with Frank Gehry on their joint proposal for a footbridge across the Thames linking St Pauls to Tate Modern, and briefly at least with Peter Eisenman on the Holocaust memorial in Berlin, he would

be extremely unlikely to do any such thing again. Indeed, Serra's relationship with Gehry has deteriorated to the point that his giant installation in the Bilbao Guggenheim can be understood as a deliberate challenge to its architectural context.

Yet the idea of collaboration continues to surface, encouraged officially by 'percentage for art' schemes and public art projects, as well as by a vague sense of obligation to unite a fractured and divided culture, and sometimes by a more committed vision about what could be possible from a genuine partnership between different cultural forms. At the same time, there is an apparent convergence between the kind of things that interest artists and the way in which architects think about what they do. Yet appearances can be deceptive. As Donald Judd was fond of saying, architecture and art may superficially look increasingly similar, but they are in fact becoming increasingly different things. But looking at the sometimes tense relationship between the two can be an important way to understand their respective priorities.

One of the more notable and, indeed, most unpredictable aspects of Future Systems' output is the range and the ambition of their work with artists. Stemming from a mixture of predisposition – Levete began her further education as an art student, while Kaplicky's father had been a notable Czech artist, who often worked with architects – personal relationships and chance, many of their projects have had a strong input from art. Or, to look at things from the other perspective, they have been invited to collaborate with an unusual number of artists, and have been able to attract artists to work with them. It is an aspect of Future Systems' work that reflects a new dimension brought by Levete to the partnership when she joined Kaplicky.

Unrealized projects include the unsuccessful submission for the competition for the Diana Princess of Wales memorial in Kensington Gardens (2002) with Anish Kapoor, a stained-glass work from Brian Clarke (1991), an artist with a particular passion for architecture, that would have formed an important aspect of two different Future Systems schemes, and a project with

351
NAPLES SUBWAY

Anthony Gormley for a bridge near the new Wembley Stadium (2004). Another design was planned with Matthew Barney in 2002, and would have taken the form of a cinema attached to Paris's Palais de Tokyo gallery for the showing of the artist's *Cremaster Cycle* – a series of films in which Richard Serra plays 'The Architect'. With the exception of their work on a temporary ice sculpture for the Snow Show with Anish Kapoor, the only project that is coming to fruition is a scheme for a subway station in Naples in collaboration with Kapoor.

These relationships have not always been easy but, despite some tensions, the results have been unusually impressive. This experience of working with artists, if nothing else, has made a visible impact on Future Systems' own work, encouraging them to become more confident about exploring the more expressive and emotional aspects of architecture, to take a less literal attitude to function and materiality. But it has also made them sharply aware of the variations in working methods and assumptions that divide artists and architects, as Levete has explained:

> As an architect, I'm used to working as part of a team … that will be made up of engineers, and accountants, and planners and clients. An artist is another person on the team for me. Artists are used to working with a singular vision. Architects have a much more complex approach. An architect's design has to work in more than just its own terms. It's a different way of conceiving and thinking from that of an artist.

The Naples project began in 2003 with an invitation from the Mayor to Kapoor to work on the building of Monte Sant'Angelo, one of the city's new generation of metro stations. Kapoor, who had earlier been introduced to

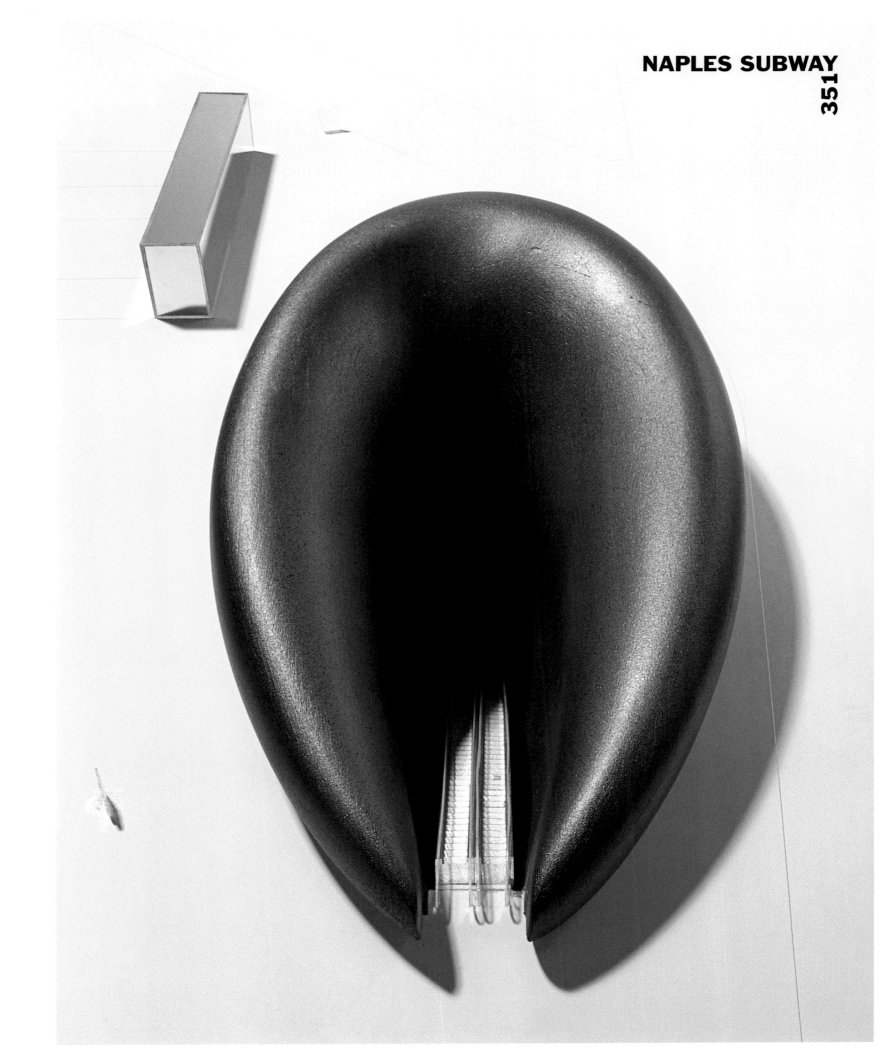

Kaplicky and Levete by Doris Saatchi, asked them for advice on how to take on a project of a complexity and scale larger than anything he had previously contemplated. They discussed the options. Kapoor could work with a local firm of Italian architects to execute his ideas, which would involve possible drawbacks in terms of a dilution of his vision, or he could either rely on Future Systems for advice, or engage in full cooperation with them. In the end they opted for that latter choice, a process that has not been without a certain amount of creative tension, but which promises to be one of the most remarkable schemes of its kind in Europe.

Before Kapoor and Future Systems started work in Naples, the underground engineering had already been completed, the escalators ordered, and a scheme designed that included two entrances, Università and Triano, located some distance apart. The strategy they adopted, which had to work within these constraints, was to emphasize the differences in character between those two entrances. The first is an expression of an underground tunnel, erupting to the surface; the second is marked by a hovering aluminium disc. One entrance is a highly polished, reflective cloud, the other has a matt, textured finish.

The tunnels themselves are rough-sprayed concrete and were originally designed to be tiled. Kapoor and Future Systems will leave them as they are: powerful,

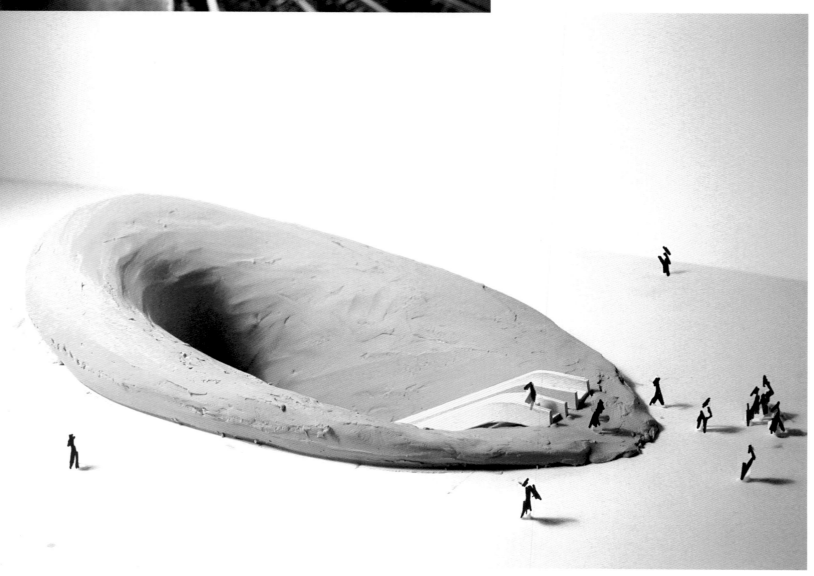

primitive and raw. With such a large-scale, outdoor project, whose budget is stretched over an enormous area, it was futile even to consider precision. 'This project is not about the control of every gesture,' says Levete:

It's not about detail. But when you do intervene, it's got to be done beautifully. The idea has to be tough enough to deal with the dirt and the rain. We're using Cor Ten and aluminium. If there's graffiti, it's either cleaned completely, or the idea is so powerful, that it doesn't matter.

Judging from the maquettes, the two very different station entrances clearly have an architectural scale and quality. Yet they are equally clearly artworks too. The process of arriving at them, and meeting the onerous technical and safety requirements of a mass-transit system, have been far from straightforward. On the one hand, the lip-like openings of the tunnel mouth have an undoubtedly sexual connotation, a reading whose impact emphasized in an earlier version by the use of mirrors to give a double hit. But they will also need to be built and detailed in such a way that they can be cleaned after a busy day in a station full of commuters, swirling dust, discarded newspapers and fast-food wrappers. As Levete puts it, 'A tiny practical detail can trip up a really good idea, and entirely negate it.' At her suggestion, the early versions of the project had a gap between the tunnel mouth and the lips. But while this was a particularly powerful arrangement from the point of view of its expressive qualities, she had to rule it out for pragmatic reasons, 'It would have been a fire hazard,' says Levete. 'There was no way in which you could have stopped rubbish from going down the cracks.' Future Systems looked at the idea from a different point of view to find a solution. 'I find that tension between the idea and the execution energizing and exciting,' says Levete 'but it can be too frustrating for an artist.'

The unsuccessful entry for the competition for a memorial to the Princess of Wales involved a different kind of collaboration with Kapoor. 'Anish rang Jan to ask to join us on the Diana team', recalls Levete:

I remember us all walking through the site on a cold Sunday morning in February. None of us had any preconceptions, but it was immediately clear to us all that we should do something on the surface of the Serpentine. For us, that was the space, rather than the park, which the other competitors used. As we saw it, the potential meaning of the fountain was so huge, and so populist, that we needed to place it on the surface of the lake, where it could be seen from many vantage points and would not get overwhelmed by sheer numbers. In that way, the edge of the water would be a place to view the memorial, and for quiet contemplation. We saw it as a swathe of white marble steps that melt and flow as they enter the water. The fountain itself would have been like a pillow of red water. At that stage we all talked a lot, and then we started to draw.

Like their collaboration in Naples, the effective realization of the creative idea depended on the resolution of the

detailed technical issues. To create the ethereal impression of a red pillow floating on the water, they would need to ensure that the structure and technical apparatus were submerged. 'We had to analyse the volume of water and the pressure that would be needed to create the pillow, and we would have had to find a way to tint the water without harming the wildlife in the Serpentine,' says Levete. In the event, the Palace's clearly expressed private preference for the Gustafsson scheme outweighed the enthusiasm of the architectural jurors for the Future Systems project.

The footbridge designed in collaboration with the artist Anthony Gormley would have formed part of the main pedestrian approach to the new stadium at Wembley. The brief was to integrate the arena with its surroundings, in particular the shops and cafés being built as part of the wider development. Future Systems worked both with Gormley and with the engineer Neil Thomas of Atelier One. The most pressing question they faced was how to address the intimidating presence of

SNOW SHOW 350

351 **Naples Subway, Monte Sant'Angelo Station, 2003**

350 **Snow Show, installation, Rovaniemi, Finland, 2003.**

the huge parabolic arch that Norman Foster has made the instantly recognisable image of the new Wembley. No amount of structural gymnastics could compete with its overwhelming strength. Their strategy was to make a bridge that would not look like a bridge, and to make a design that was not a design. They worked on the idea of creating a kind of concrete landscape that did not have an entirely predetermined form. 'We wanted to make a shape by pouring truck-loads of molten concrete into a cage of reinforcing steel,' says Levete.

Preparing for the presentation, the team realized that it was not a proposition that could be modelled satisfactorily. 'We had to do it for real, so we worked in Gormley's studio and experimented.' The idea of a concrete pour suggests solidity, but from a technical point of view, Future Systems thought about describing the form as if it were an inflatable skin. As Levete describes it:

> We were working with what is really a heavy, crude material and trying to see what happens when it is captured by a delicate net of stainless steel. We wanted to look at what we could do to polish the surface, and create a deck. Gormley said, "This is not my language," but he had mocked up five different versions of how the material could work. We wanted to create a barrier and make something that looked like a lava flow, to make it seem deliberately artificial, and not too literal.

In the event, Future Systems' project was rejected by the developer, but it got far enough to demonstrate the unusual and perhaps unexpected degree of ambition that they bring to their collaborations with major figures from the world of contemporary art.

**327 Diana Memorial,
London, 2002.**

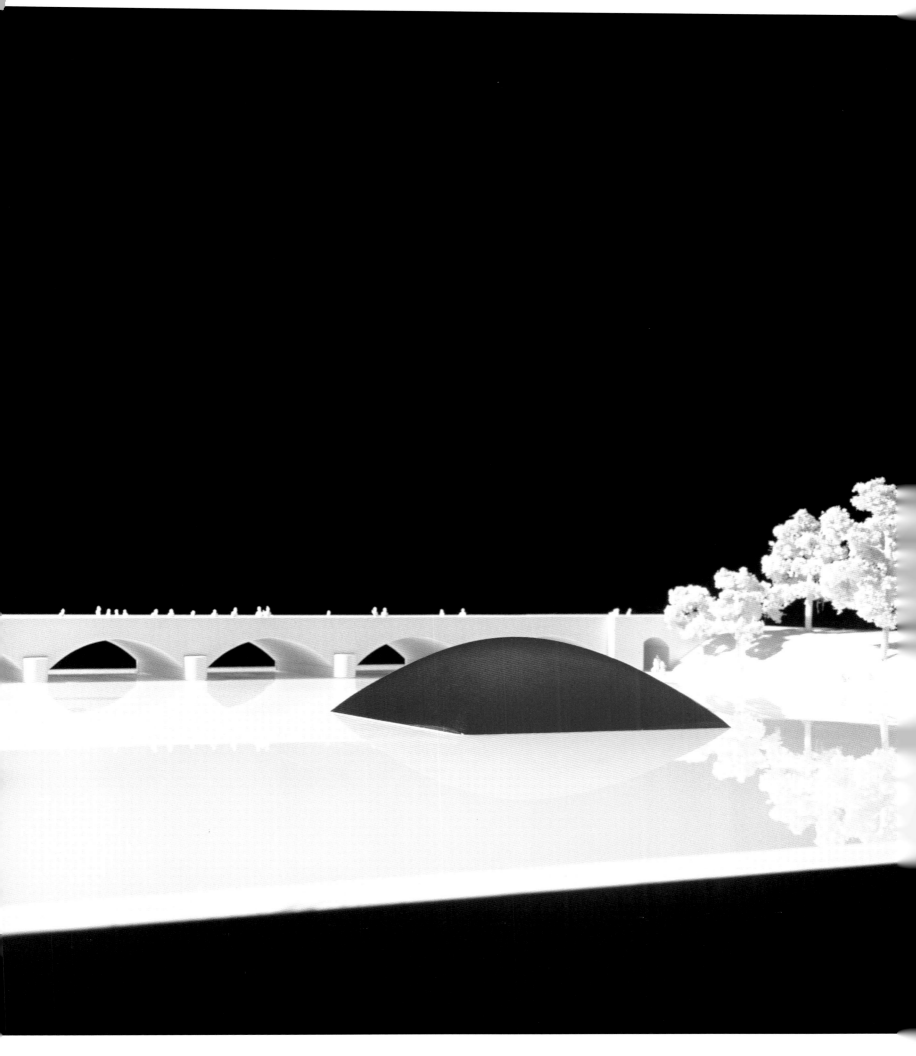

A building has to last,

it can't be just about fashion Jan Kaplicky

F or better or worse, the museum has a pressing claim to be regarded as the most revealing of building types in the architecture of the last decade. It is certainly the most conspicuous. We may try to convince ourselves that it is new building technologies, or the impact of digitization on design, green questions, or social housing and urbanism, that are the issues that frame architectural discourse, rather than attention-grabbing shapes. But more often than not we see the museum as the distillation of architectural time passing. It is a building type on which an extraordinary amount of design energy has been invested. Perhaps only the individual house or, more recently, the born-again high-rise, can challenge its stubborn grip on the architectural and critical imagination.

'You sometimes hear people say that the museum is out of date,' says Kaplicky:

I don't accept that. You hear it said about libraries and exhibitions too. Its not true. The museum is one form that will survive; it's a chance to do something unusual. The museum and the artefact will not disappear. A work of art or a motor car can't be replaced by an image on a screen, it's a totally different experience.

Museums have become signature structures that are used to define the character of cities, and provide a surrogate for a public realm that is threatened by the privatization of more traditional forms of public space. Part of the point for every architect commissioned to

create such a project is to produce a design that does not look like other museums. There are enough technical issues imposed by the need for correct light levels, the protection of artworks from the destructive effect of sunshine, and the impact of circulation routes, to provide architects with all the raw material they need to make a building with depth and complexity, but not so many as to get in the way of sculptural invention. A museum does not usually have the wide range of spatial and technical needs of a school, say – a building type that Future Systems have recently begun to address – with its complicated functional relationships, its acoustic and daylight issues, and its demand for a cellular layout. (Future Systems have worked on both small and large-scale education projects. They began with an experimental classroom scheme in 2001 – a pod-like addition to an existing school aimed at encouraging learning – before moving on to planning complete schools.) Nor does a museum impose the technical demands of a stadium, fundamentally a giant machine for getting people in and out as quickly and as safely as possible, and offering as many seats with unimpeded views of the ground as is practicable. Unlike these buildings, a museum can in many cases essentially be shaped by architects and their aesthetic ambitions. Because the size of the artworks that a museum can be expected to contain have grown rapidly in recent years, so has the scale of the museum. At the same time, it has a highly public, representational

role that has also encouraged the building of ever-larger structures.

Future Systems have explored the nature of the museum through a series of architectural competitions and self-generated research studies. And they have brought to it a perhaps unexpectedly sober perspective. With such robust building types as the department store, Future Systems have been highly inventive about shape-making, and have made bold experiments with colour and the use of unfamiliar materials. But in their museum projects they have been careful to maintain the primacy of the museological object, at least in the interior. They have been ready to treat architecture as background rather than foreground, pulling back to allow the visitor to experience the exhibit with a minimum of intrusive detail.

The exception is their unsuccessful competition proposal for an addition to the Natural History Museum in London, designed in flamboyant high Victorian Lombardy gothic by Alfred Waterhouse. In 1985 Future Systems conceived an equally flamboyant extension, and used an even more vivid colour palette. Levete explains this by drawing a distinction between the museum's collection, its particular display techniques and those that would be used by an art museum. 'It was overstating the point architecturally. We understood the extension as being seen as a twist on the original museum's architecture. The things you would have been going to see are so contained and so specific that you could afford to overstate the building.'

318 World Classrooms, London, 2001.

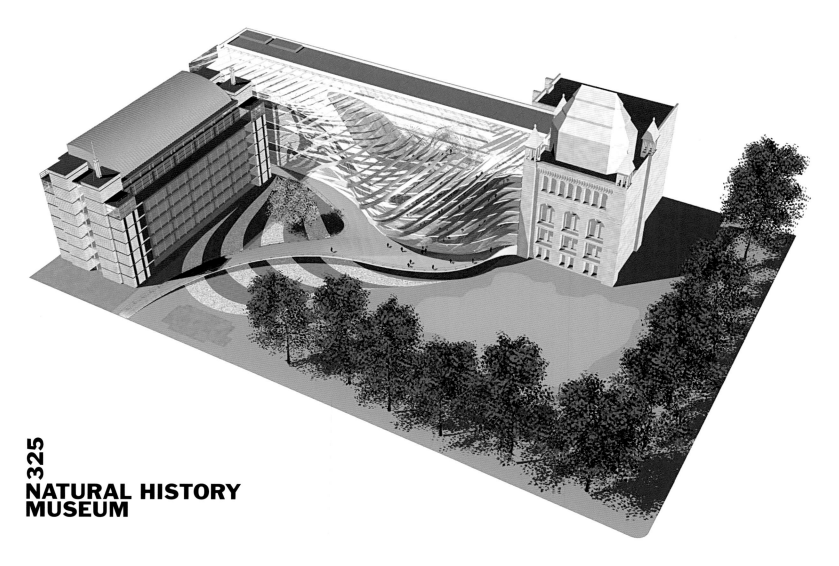

325
NATURAL HISTORY MUSEUM

In other Future Systems museum projects, the critical design issues on which they have focused have been the relationship of display systems to architecture, and the balance of artificial and natural light, as well as the elimination of intrusive structural elements. Future Systems has shown a continuing preference for the physical, as opposed to the virtual experience in display methods, despite the radical nature of its architecture. Kaplicky's attitudes to the relationship of art to the museum context are unexpectedly gentle. The simplicity of the original Museum of Modern Art in New York, which he first saw in the 1960s, left a particular impression. 'The interiors were never in competition with the art, and the garden was a masterpiece.' Kaplicky was also deeply impressed by the sight of the museum's Bell Jet Ranger helicopter, hanging inside the design gallery.

Another influence was Max Gordon, an architect who was himself a significant collector of art. When Kaplicky first met him in the 1970s, they were both working on the design of the Brighton Marina in the office of the Louis de Soissons partnership. Gordon went on to design the original Saatchi Gallery in London (1985). He helped Kaplicky crystallize his thinking about art. 'The keys to an architecturally successful gallery are the floor and the lights; nothing else matters as much.' Peter Zumthor's Kunsthaus (1997) in Bregenz also impressed Future

Systems. 'I have never seen Anish Kapoor's work look better,' says Kaplicky. Additionally, he speaks unexpectedly warmly of Carlo Scarpa, not necessarily because of the architectural language that he used, but because of his boldness in creating a fresh approach to the display of ancient artefacts. With their startling juxtapositions of contemporary simplicity – and jewel-like precision – with the baroque or gothic fragments of art, Scarpa's display techniques were an inspiration.

Scarpa was the revolutionary who first managed to exhibit pieces of art from different periods in a modern way, in the big Italian palazzos. He was a master. The elegance of how you display objects is critical. Scarpa had a way of showing gothic objects that was not polite, but which was beautiful.

For Amanda Levete, who has a personal preference for smaller, more scholarly gallery spaces, such as the Wallace Collection in London, the Musée du Jeu de Pomme in Paris and New York's Frick Collection, art galleries should be prepared to exhibit a certain reticence. 'I don't like galleries that become a spectacle in themselves,' she says. And she voices a preference for Tate Britain over Tate Modern. 'I used to love being alone in the room with the Rothkos in the old Tate. I go to a gallery to be alone with my thoughts, I don't go there to

325 **Natural History Museum, London, 2001.**

172 New Acropolis Museum,
Athens, 1990.

172
**NEW ACROPOLIS
MUSEUM**

335 **Egyptian Museum**, Giza, 2002.

The keys to an architecturally successful gallery are the floor and the lights, nothing else matters as much

Jan Kaplicky

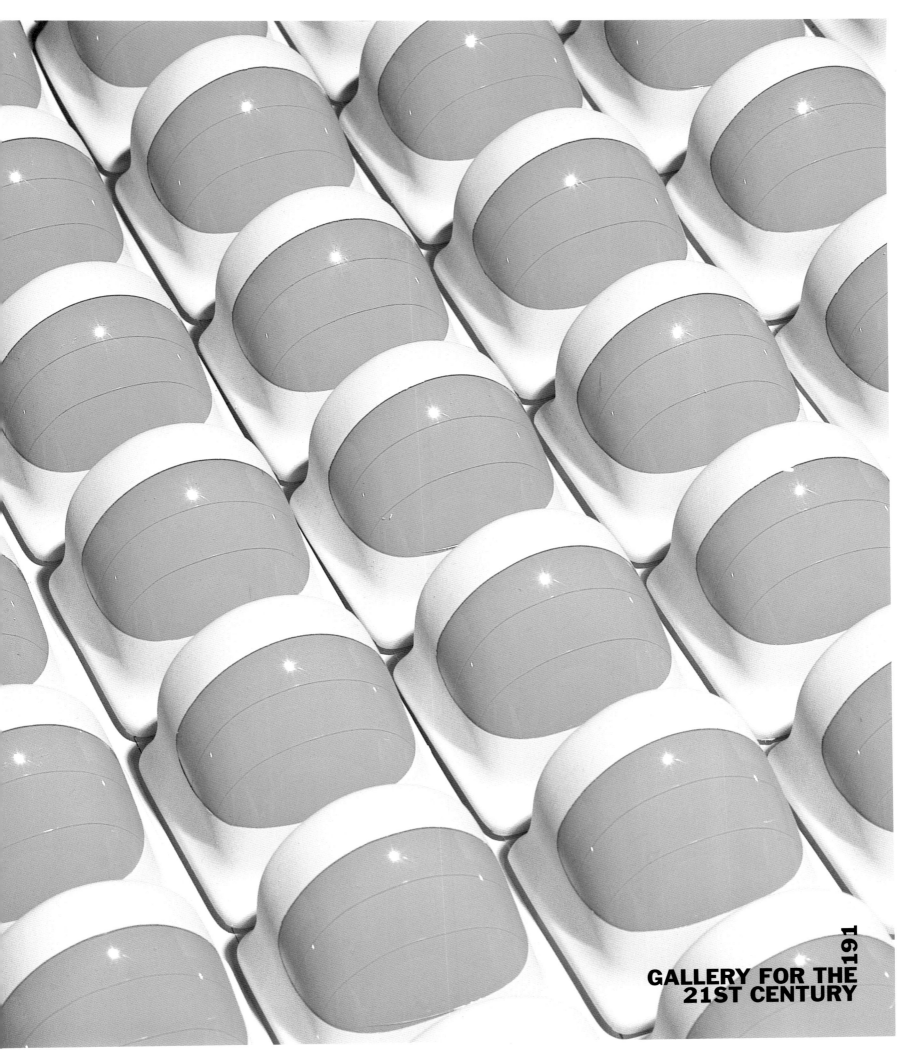

**GALLERY FOR THE
21ST CENTURY**

be with people. Galleries are not about people-watching for me.' She predicts a backlash against exhibitionistic museums, and a return to a more modest approach in their design.

Future Systems have explored, at one extreme, the design of museums that have involved accommodating some of the greatest collections of archaeological fragments of the classical period, and some much more modestly scaled exhibition projects. They have designed galleries for collections of contemporary art, as well as a blue and gold glass museum of ancient Egyptian culture, and a café housed in a gold conning tower with a view of the pyramids. It is a sequence that has made them particularly sensitive to the tension between content and container that is an essential issue to be resolved in the design of any museum. Their theoretical studies culminated in a commission for the construction of a new museum for the Maserati collection of historic cars in Modena, a project won in competition after a couple of more modest designs for the Italian high-performance luxury-car builder created a relationship with the company. When complete, it will be the first museum that Future Systems have built.

The Maserati Museum design clearly has its roots in the sequence of museum projects that began back in 1990, when Future Systems took part in the competition for the design of a new museum in Athens to house the archaeological collection relating to the Parthenon, and, by implication, to provide a home for the contested Parthenon marbles in the unlikely event that the British Museum should ever consent to their return to Greece. Future Systems did not win, and in fact the victorious project was itself abandoned. A second competition, staged much later, was won by Bernard Tschumi. That project also faced difficulties and delays, suggesting just how politically complicated the building of a museum on such a highly charged site can be. The Parthenon Museum is as much a question of national identity as it is of technical issues, but for Future Systems the Athens submission was also a significant step that helped to crystallize their approach both to museums and to the architectural context.

Competitors were offered a choice of three sites. Future Systems opted to build on the one that was being used as a restaurant, an area of land nearest the monument that was judged to be free of archaeological remains. No architectural project could have been conceived for a more historically sensitive setting than this one, under the gaze of the white marble walls of the greatest monument of Periclean Athens. Even the most self-absorbed of architects could not conceive of deliberately designing a museum in competition with Ictinus's masterwork. Yet the contents of the museum are in themselves extraordinary pieces of art, and deserve to be treated with the appropriate respect. A museum to accommodate them cannot therefore be entirely invisible: it must have a certain presence and character of its own if it is to reflect the value that we place on its contents. It should unobtrusively put visitors in an appropriate frame of mind for approaching the

364
COLCHESTER
VISUAL ARTS

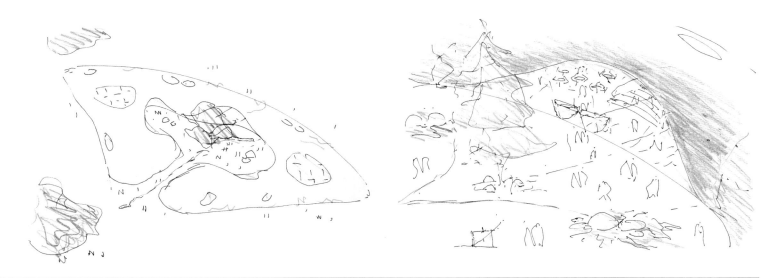

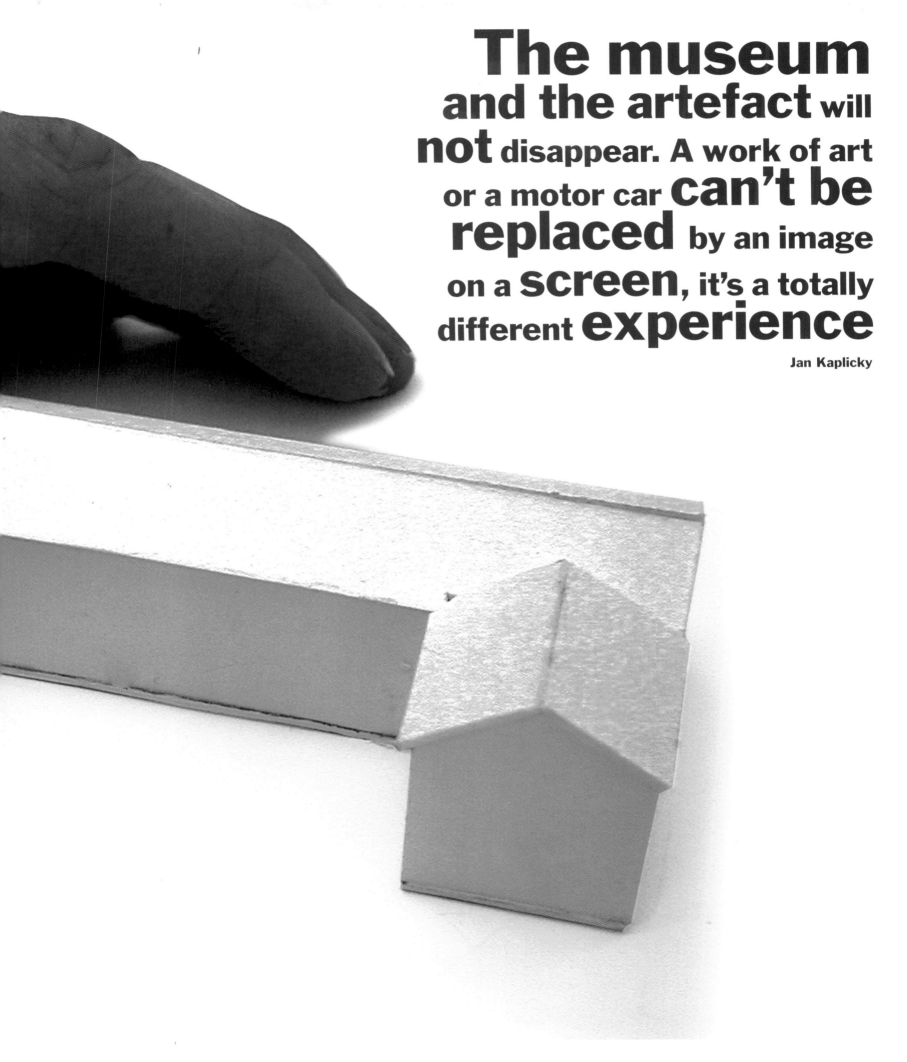

The museum and the artefact will **not** disappear. A work of art or a motor car **can't be replaced** by an image on a **screen**, it's a totally different **experience**

Jan Kaplicky

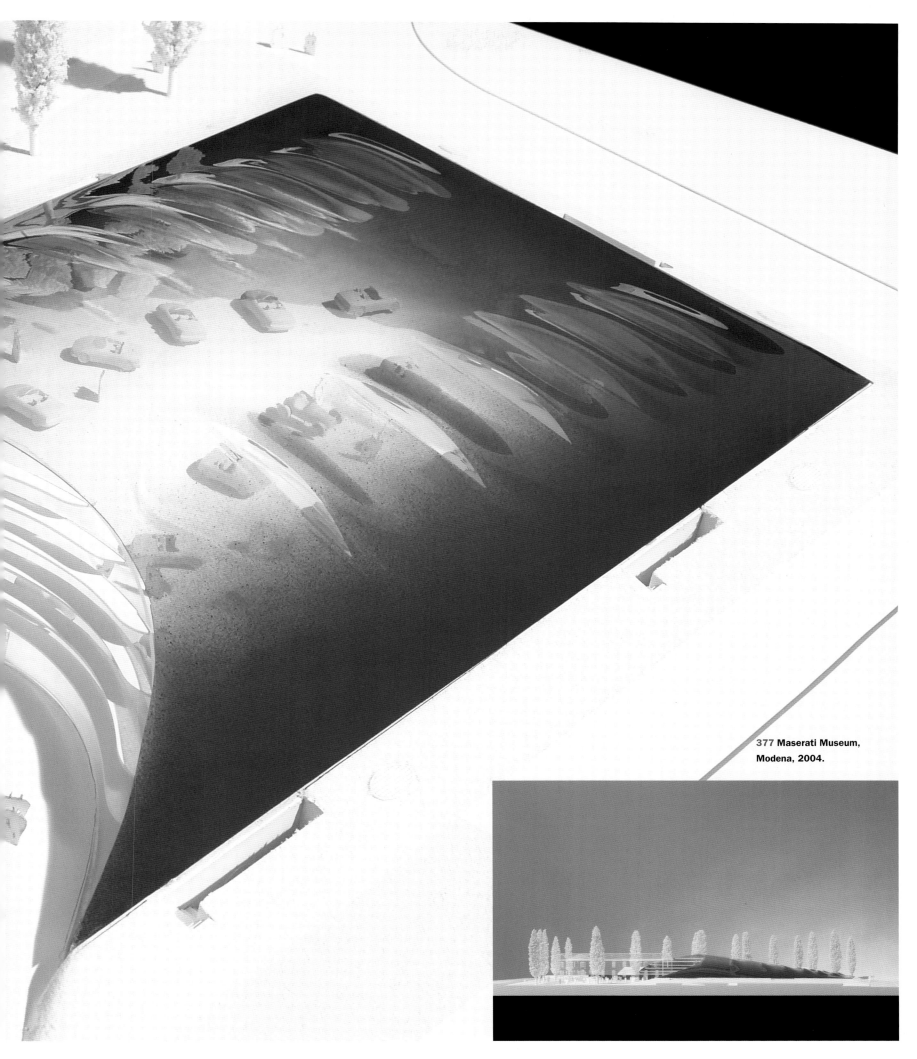

377 Maserati Museum, Modena, 2004.

377 Maserati Museum, Modena, 2004.

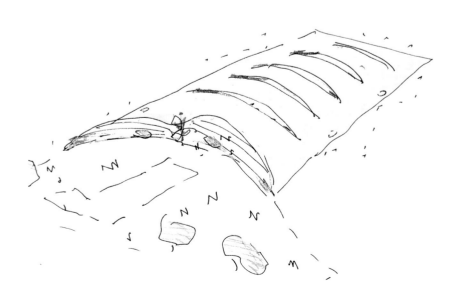

exhibits, and give them the best possible viewing conditions. That is why an underground structure – the least intrusive solution from the point of view of context – seemed inappropriate. However, Future Systems considered daylight essential to creating the right conditions for viewing the sculptures, which were originally carved to be seen bathed in Athenian sunshine, and thus they opted for the extensive use of glass. The museum, as Future Systems saw it, had to take its place in the landscape. It was designed not only to highlight the exhibits, but also to establish their continuing relationship with the Parthenon from which they came, and to give viewers the best chance of understanding them in that context.

The question of what constitutes the most appropriate form of architectural expression for a museum designed to contain some of the most powerful surviving remnants of classical culture anywhere in the world (which was also an issue for the project that Future Systems worked on for a museum of Egyptian archaeology within a few kilometres of the pyramids) is not one that has a straightforward answer. Deference is certainly the primary requirement. But there are different interpretations of the nature of architectural deference. In such a context, to refer to the language of classicism could be understood as a form of impertinence, or even parody, diminishing both monument and artefacts through conspicuous inauthenticity. 'Put the exhibits in a neo-classical building, and they are lost; they take on an entirely different meaning,' says Kaplicky.

Future Systems' strategy was to render the museum building as invisible and as unassertive as possible by making it as little like a traditional piece of architecture as they could, in the belief that this would give the monument the space, both physical and conceptual, that it deserves. The container would not read as a building, but could be understood almost as a naturally occurring form, like a cloud, or a glass hill, rather than a self-conscious piece of architectural shape-making. For

Future Systems this was the route towards achieving the gentlest possible relationship between old and new. A slender ribbon bridge would have connected the museum with the path leading towards the Acropolis, offering a continuous view of the monument as visitors approached. The museum structure would take the form of a flowing sequence of glass curves, spilling naturally out of the ground. Like an architectural stealth bomber, it would be off the radar screens of visibility. The precise lines of the gentle, low, curved forms did not come easily. The eventual inspiration was the lip of a classical Greek theatre cut into a hillside, which seemed to offer the most satisfactory relationship with the ground.

The intention with the design of the architectural container was to give meaning to the objects. In particular, the museum was designed to provide a scale that would not risk turning heroic architectural fragments into toys or decorative trivia, but would help them to retain some of the original meaning that they had had in the open air. This was the result of a trip to see the marbles in the British Museum, when Kaplicky and Levete came away with the impression that they looked lost in a space without the sense of scale that would define them. Instead, Future Systems conceived the surfaces on which the artefacts would be displayed with as much sophistication as the architecture of the building.

The Parthenon Museum's low, curved shapes provided the unifying theme for a series of designs for museums that was to follow, from which their proposed addition to Alfred Waterhouse's Natural History Museum in London, an extravagant Grade One-listed gothic building, was a notable exception. The connecting bridge is another recurring theme, originating in the Athens project, which was to be explored in several subsequent proposals, including the French National Library competition and their scheme for Tate at London's Bankside.

For Kaplicky, the challenge is to make the optimum space to show art, which for him is not one in which architectural bombast has driven out art. The challenge, he believes, would involve creating a new paradigm for gallery architecture. When the Tate Gallery was looking for a new home for its modern collection, Future Systems worked on a polemical proposal for what they called a 'Gallery for the 21st Century' that showed what might be possible if, rather than adapting the existing Bankside power station, which it had just started to consider, the Tate had decided to start from a blank sheet of paper, and build an entirely new museum.

The design involved a proposal for a bridge across the Thames, long before the competition to build one was won by Norman Foster and Anthony Caro. But for Future Systems the real priority was the creation of an entirely top-lit exhibition space with no heavy structural elements to get in the way of the art, and to create an outstanding sculpture garden. 'When you're designing an exhibition, top-lit space is always on your mind,' say Future Systems:

But you have to be careful. Mies van der Rohe's gallery in Berlin has a seven metre high space on the ground floor, which looks fantastic, and dramatic, but it doesn't work for the art. Only a very few special pieces can be shown in spaces like that. There is a problem with a lot of gallery architecture. The display systems some architects produce are very often on the crudest, almost primitive level. Artists, on the other hand, like an old, or a semi-old environment. They think it looks better and they don't like modern architectural spaces, which they think interfere with the art. The result at the new Tate is that some of the spaces are enfilade with 3:5 proportions, just like the rooms in an old castle.

Future Systems were determined to address the issue of display systems in a radical way. The starting point was the lighting conditions for objects both large and small. The scheme treated the gallery as a gentle staircase, rising in shallow steps under the shelter of a glass roof that would have supported a network of hoods, designed to filter out everything but north light. A second set of filters on the south side of the hood would have served to transfer the light down into the interior. At the same time, the design avoided creating a sequence of rooms for the display. For Future Systems this would have been too limiting a response, which would be at odds with the architectural character of the museum, and its contents. And it would have imposed too prescriptive a means of viewing and understanding the collection as a linear series of objects that could not be seen in space. Instead, Future Systems looked to provide a family of related forms in sophisticated materials. These would have been shown in the context of a fluid series of spaces that encouraged movement through the whole building. Orientation was also a key issue. 'You always see the river, and the sky. The old Saatchi Gallery was a continuous open space, where you could experience three rooms at once. The Tate should have views too.'

Future Systems' unbuilt scheme for a small, civic museum in Colchester demonstrates a further application of their thinking about display techniques:

The partitions are temporary, they move, and so they can't be architecture. Continuity interests me. When you're working with small exhibition rooms that may contain six or eight paintings, you don't see the next one. If the art moves from the walls to three-dimensional objects and sculpture, you need different kinds of spaces, not just rooms. And then if you're working on a display of contemporary art, how do you show or store video? Most screens remind you of a domestic situation, or they become just another cinema, or one of those video walls in shops that nobody looks at any more.

Colchester's new museum would have been just 5,000 m², and was intended to address both the needs of a collection of art accommodated in a small house, and the urbanistic problems of the chosen site, facing a small park. The exhibitions were allocated one third of

377 Maserati Museum, Modena, 2004.

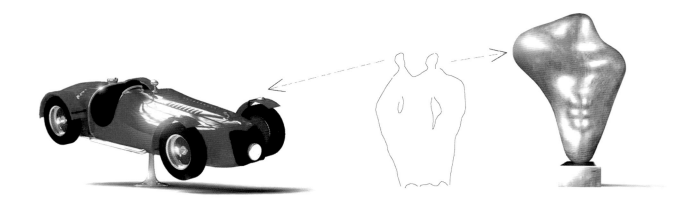

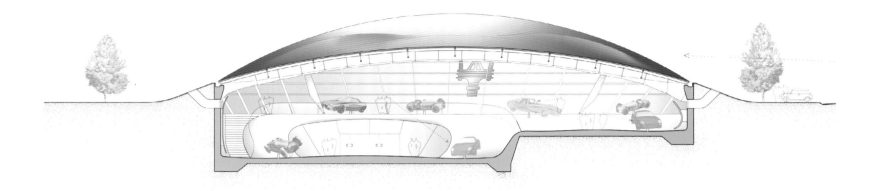

377 Maserati Museum,
Modena, 2004.

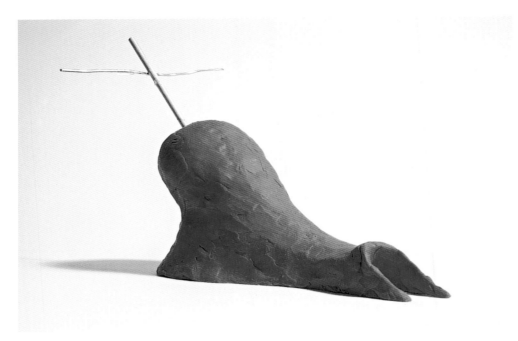

LISBON CHURCH
366

366 Lisbon Church,
concept project, 2004.

the space; the rest would have been used as a social centre, planned around a courtyard, with one huge tree. The gallery on the top floor would have used a version of the partitions devised for Future Systems' 'Gallery of the 21st Century'. The structure would have included louvres, with flaps opened up by hand to adjust for winter and summer, so as to block the southern light. The overall design marked the end of a certain line of development, moving beyond blob-like forms and towards a more hybrid geometry that includes straight lines as well as fluid shapes. Future Systems' work on the gallery has eventually led to a commission, which is on its way to being realized. They have also worked on a new approach to the design of libraries, demonstrated by their entry for the competition for a new public library in Rouen. Here, digitally controlled storage systems allow for an economic and very different use of space and form.

As yet, however, Future Systems have not put the idea into practice.

The Selfridges department store in Birmingham can be seen as the fulfilment of two decades of speculation about new ways of dealing with the insertion of substantial contemporary buildings into urban sites, while the Lords Media Centre is the realization of an equally long interest in the possibilities of semi-monocoque structures. The Maserati Museum is the closest that Future Systems has come so far to realizing a museum with the deft, stealthy quality that they have proposed for various sites around the world.

The museum is designed for a site adjoining the old farmhouse that was once the home of the great car engineer, Enzio Ferrari. Maserati's factory is nearby. The Maserati and Ferrari enterprises both have the same parent company; they are part of the Fiat group, controlled by Luca di Montezemolo, a businessman with an interest in every area of design, from furniture to fashion. And it is part of his strategy to nurture the lustre of Maserati's heritage, which lost some direction as a result of going through the hands of a series of different owners in the 1970s and 1980s. Since Fiat took it on, it has invested in new models, in new production lines and now in the museum, which is intended to add to the aura surrounding one of the most famous names of Italian engineering. The building itself will be a highly visible sign of the company's new strategy, a landmark bordered by the high-speed rail line entering Modena, and a sign of its new investment. The new museum is part of a strategy to celebrate the heritage of the marque, and to help promote it to a new generation. The cars that Ferrari raced personally will be inside the old workshop, while the new museum, collecting historic material that is at present spread around the world, will tell the story of Maserati through a sequence of cars and other artefacts.

Shaped like a car bonnet, the Maserati Museum is planned around a display of twenty-eight vehicles, from various years. The entrance is through a glass wall, smoothly fitted into the hull of the structure like a car radiator. Once inside, you can look back and see Ferrari's house through the glass, which is itself treated as a kind of exhibit. Interior and exterior are tied together by a single terrazzo floor finish that would even be used inside the house, glossy for the interiors and more subdued outdoors. The technical problems posed by the impact of oil dripping from still-active car engines will possibly be resolved with something as straightforward as a tray to collect the drips. The ceramic-tile finish will link interior with exterior, connecting the new structure with Ferrari's old house.

The building's skin, made from extruded aluminium panelling, will suggest the precision of auto engineering, and is considerably more sophisticated than the straightforward steel portal structure that will support it. But it is made to disappear from view. On the inside, it is masked by a stretched-fabric diffusing screen, on the outside, by the cladding, in the manner of the Selfridges project in Birmingham, which makes a similar division between eye-catching surface and workmanlike substructure. From the exterior, the sweeping curves emerge like a soap bubble directly out of the turfed landscape, as if in memory of the lip of the amphitheatre that had inspired Future Systems' earlier Parthenon Museum. Inside, the museum is a single, undifferentiated space, apart from the bookshop and the restaurant, which are accommodated in twin blisters, bulging out of the wall on either side of the structure. The building itself, which Kaplicky calls a non-building, will read as a kind of subliminal billboard. The interior walls are used for most of the exhibition information, concentrated in a ribbon band, while the cars will be shown as sculptures, isolated in space, lit by clusters of light fittings in the ceiling.

In designing a museum to house a collection of cars, Future Systems have worked hard to overcome the association of displaying historic vehicles with a car showroom, or a garage. A convention has taken root in many car museums whereby the vehicles are simply parked and fenced in by a thick, tasselled rope, threaded through the kind of brass fence posts that you might find outside a nightclub. They are usually positioned too close to each other for spectators to get a complete view. 'It must not look like a car park,' the designers comment, 'so the cars are mounted at a tilt and are all elevated on a pivot to allow you to see the chassis. They are also given the space to be seen as sculptural objects in space.' This is achieved through a kind of undercarriage, like that of the Le Corbusier chaise longue, which angles the cars, giving them a heightened presence. And crucially, it has given the cars room to breathe. They are remarkably powerful objects, colourful, richly detailed, and complex, combining exquisite mechanical detail and carefully considered control panels with an overall form that, while it is designed with high performance in mind, clearly also has an emotional and expressive content.

The museum itself is the height of visual discretion, like an aircraft wing that hides electrical and hydraulic systems and structure in a slender, all but invisible, but still beautiful form that does not compete in any way with the cars that it is sheltering and putting on display. The cars will be shown in different configurations, some with a door left open to leave the dashboard visible. Accompanying photographs, texts and artefacts will be grouped in a wall display with a minimum of video content. The roof is a steel structure, spanning across a concrete basin floor, with simple steel and aluminium elements forming the interior.

375 Rouen Library, 2004.

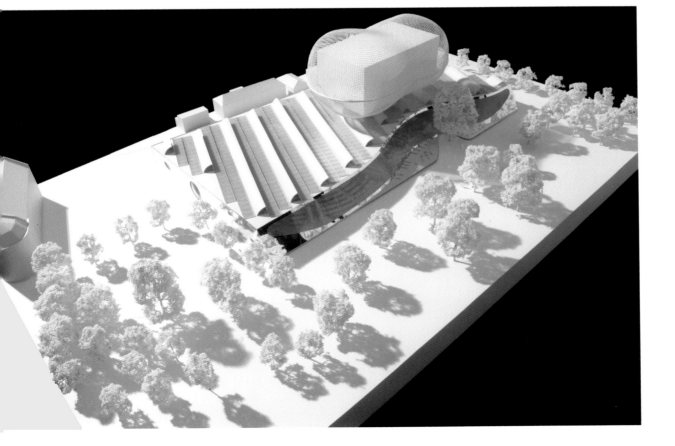

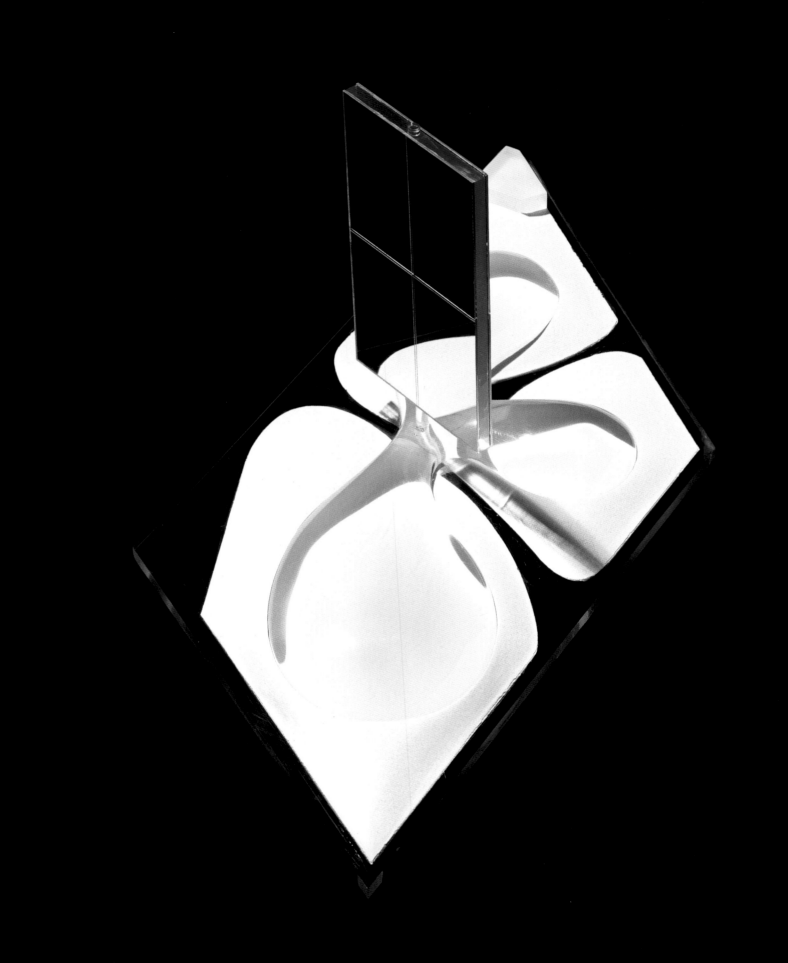

331 Library Birmingham, 2002

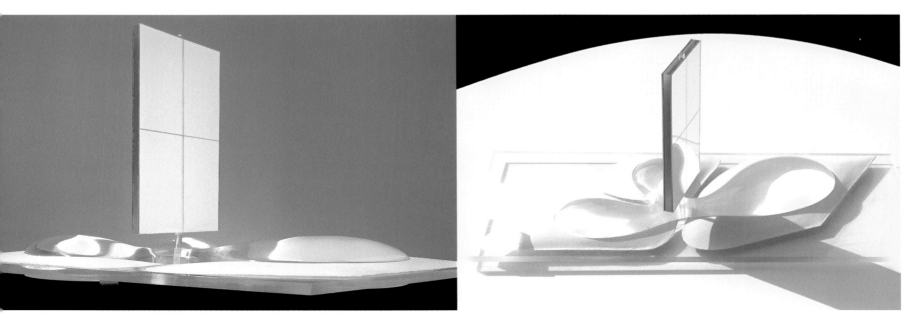

Bridges are about engineering, but there is a lot of art in them too.

Don't try and tell me that it is all about mathematics

Jan Kaplicky

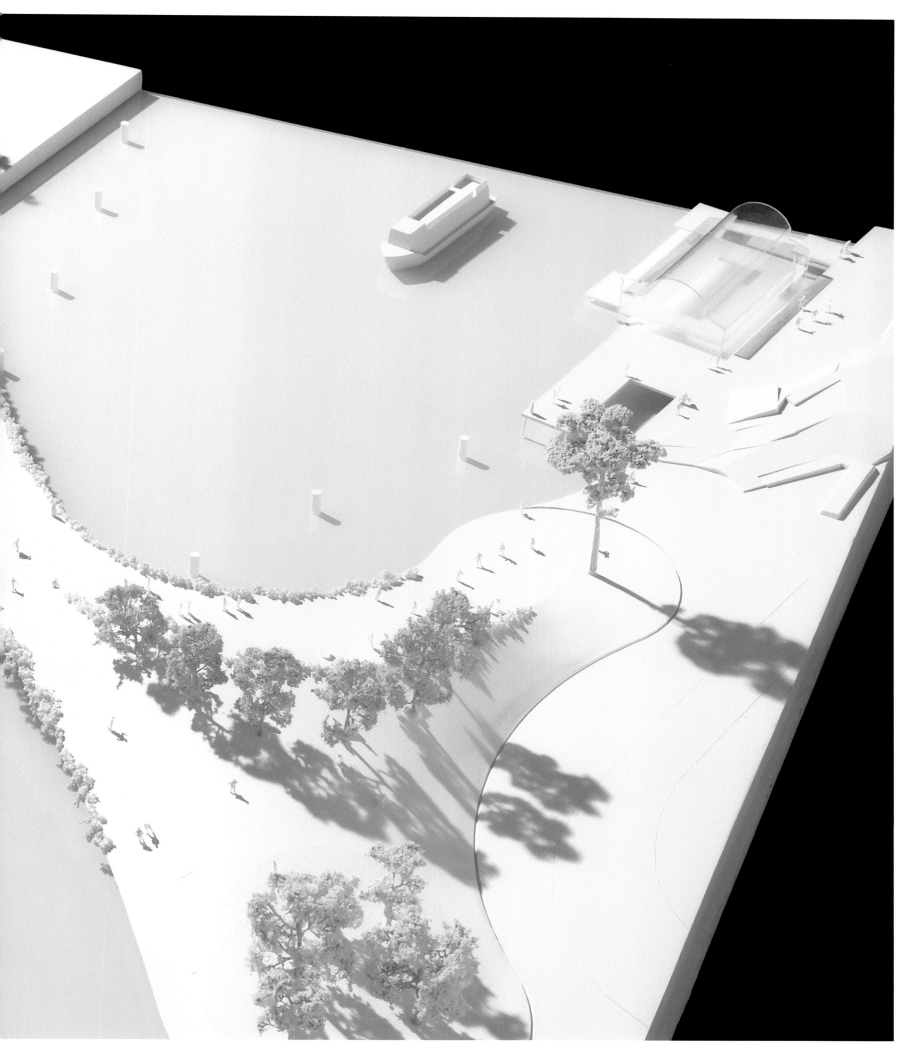

ne of the more surprising architectural developments of the last decade has been the extension of the architect's repertoire to encompass the bridge. This shift in responsibility from engineer to architect has resulted in an unexpectedly sudden transformation. The archetypal bridge has gone from being the kind of structure in which the highest goal was to make it as invisible and as unemphatic as possible, into one where the principal apparent objective is a celebration of the act of crossing the void. Twenty years ago a successful bridge was one that spanned the greatest possible distance with the least visible effort. Arches were flattened, support structures minimized, structure merged imperceptibly with superstructure. And economy of means counted for a lot. Now, the more elaborately ingenious, the more conspicuous and the more exhibitionistic the structure the better. The shift is not the product of technical developments, except in as far as a dramatic increase in the power of computing analysis has made more complex approaches much more readily achievable. The new generation of bridges rarely relies on new construction methods or materials. The variation in their form is a reflection of changing taste and has been heavily influenced by the work of the engineer-architect Santiago Calatrava, who designed a particularly striking series of bridges in the early 1990s. As Kaplicky says, you have to look at bridges in terms of before Calatrava and after. The result is the development of the pedestrian bridge, in particular, as a kind of minor art form, pitched far beyond the scale of the domestic object, and with more of a functional burden than Future Systems' artistic collaborations, but still with fewer practical demands on their design than those imposed by what might be called 'mainstream' architecture.

Kaplicky's early memories of Czechoslovakia have provided a rich source of imagery and inspiration for his bridge designs. He talks about the impact made on him by the Charles Bridge in Prague, with baroque statues standing on its parapets, as well as the impression left by the daring structural engineering of the pioneers of the 1930s, and by the older legacy of Eiffel.

For Future Systems designing a bridge is an opportunity to explore the imaginative possibilities of structural design. 'A bridge, especially a pedestrian bridge, leaves a designer free. The major constraint is disabled access; a ramp would be structurally feasible, but the regulations rule it out,' says Kaplicky. 'The power of a bridge is in its elegance, in how it lets you cross, and in that, the surface is critical.' It can also be the starting point for the possibility of introducing unfamiliar extra elements to the usual ingredients of a conventional bridge, as in Future

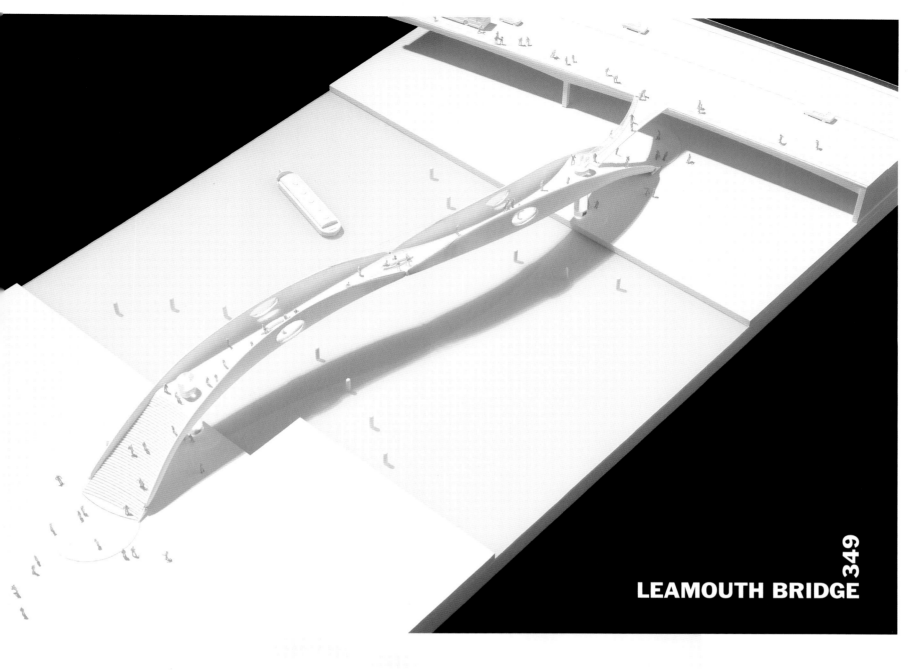

349 Leamouth Bridge,
London, 2003.

Systems' scheme for Wembley Stadium's approaches in collaboration with Anthony Gormley.

But Future Systems' first detailed proposition for a bridge was an unrealized design for a foot bridge in Croydon (1993). It was part of a series of proposals for a civic improvement campaign aimed at countering Croydon's grey image, and would have involved a mast-and-cable supported arrangement. Future Systems' design for a Clyde crossing in Glasgow would have put a park on the bridge deck, while the scheme for the Leamouth bridge on an east London tributary of the Thames required a structure organized in three distinct pieces, supported on two piers to deal with level changes and other obstacles. They have worked on major structural crossings, as well as more exotic ideas such as a speculative design to replace the existing wooden

Accademia bridge crossing Venice's Grand Canal, a project inspired by Oscar Niemeyer's design for the same spot. The problem here, apart from the remarkable setting, is the need to integrate sufficient clearance for canal traffic. Future Systems' design concentrates on integrating a stepped ramp into a curved, smooth shell form, taking its shape from a gondola hull. For Kaplicky, what the bridge looks like from underneath is as much an issue as the view in profile.

Future Systems have one striking, realized bridge to their credit so far, and many more unbuilt designs. Even before they had completed a major building, they had successfully finished a pedestrian bridge at Canary Wharf, built as part of the development's investment in pedestrian infrastructure and the public realm. The brief reflected many of their preoccupations with prefabrication

400 Venice Bridge, concept project, 2005.

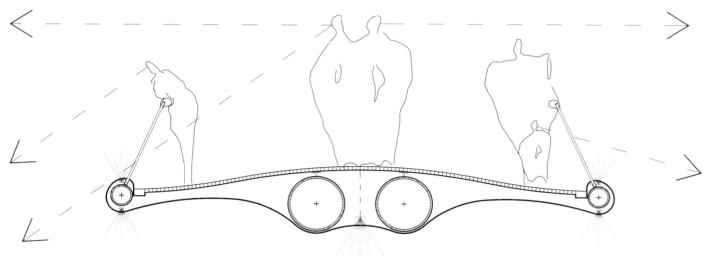

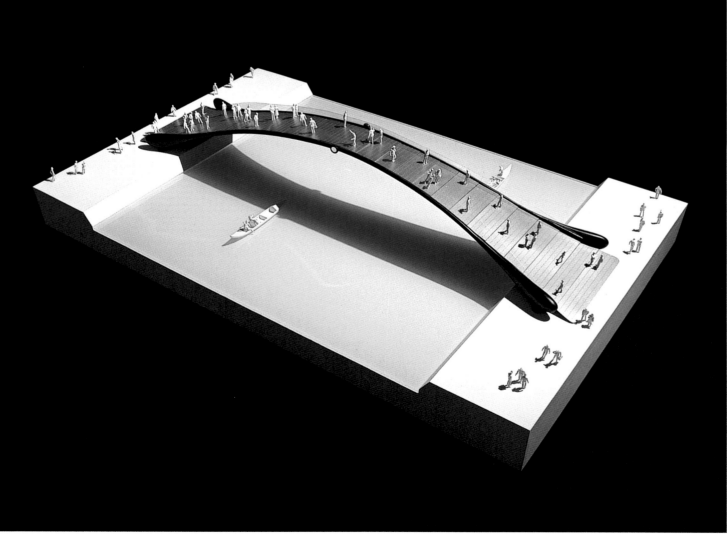

FLOATING BRIDGE

219 **Floating Bridge,**
London, 1994.

and portability. The structure needed to be lightweight to avoid imposing more than a minimal load on the Victorian wharf side; it needed to be prefabricated to minimize site disruption and speed up the installation process, and it had to be capable of opening up in the middle for occasional shipping. Their solution was a floating pontoon bridge, part preassembled and then floated into position for a final assembly that required no piles. The delicate skeletal structure, finished in vivid lime green, sat on top of a sequence of floats, providing a distinctive but economical solution.

The structure was designed as two 35 metre sections that were fabricated at a yard in Littlehampton and driven up overnight in a special convoy. The pontoons, based on the approach adopted for temporary military bridges, were simple drums, filled with polystyrene to give them the buoyancy that would make them unsinkable in even the most difficult circumstances. The time spent at the site installing the bridge was just two weeks.

Since then, Future Systems have designed a whole range of bridges on a variety of scales. Bridges have formed an integral part of many of the studio's architectural projects – including their schemes for the French National Library in Paris and Tate Modern in London. The architect's role in designing a bridge is an essentially ambiguous one. The engineer is in theory in a position to produce the most logical, elegant and economical structure without architects. Few architects could build a bridge without an engineer. 'Bridges are about engineering, but there is a lot of art in them too. Don't try and tell me that it is all about mathematics,' says Kaplicky. 'Of course there are rules, but a bridge has to be about intuition too.' For Future Systems, the role of the architect in designing a bridge is to demand more of engineers, to push them into looking at things in new ways and at a different scale. It is also to encourage them to explore unfamiliar techniques. In Britain, for example, concrete remained underdeveloped as a material for bridge design when compared with mainland Europe until comparatively recently. It took the arrival of such distinguished continental engineers as the German Felix Samuely to change that picture. Kaplicky still laments the conservatism in Britain among bridge builders, which has, for instance, hindered the realization of a major aluminum bridge. 'Even Owen Williams' buildings were very very simple,' says Kaplicky. 'When you look at the M1 bridges, the parapets are so clunky, it seems as if they're from the 1920s, when they were actually built in the 1950s.'

Kaplicky acknowledges the ambiguities of the relationship between an architect and an engineer working together on designing a bridge:

You want support from an engineer and you can't give them impossible problems. Maybe my designs are too much like engineering, and some engineers don't like that. But I can't dimension a beam on my own and, in any case, engineering is not really about calculation, it's a philosophy, and that is what can reduce a dimension of 100 cm down to 80 cm. For an architect, choosing an engineer is based on developing a sense of trust, of course. And at Future Systems, we have worked with many good engineers: Tony Hunt, Frank Newby, Peter Rice, Jiri Strasky and others. You need an individual relationship.

For Kaplicky, successful bridges depend on the right partnership with the right engineer. 'If you're lucky, you'll find them. Oscar Niemeyer always depended on just two or three engineers who could do concrete for him.'

**219 Floating Bridge,
London, 1994.**

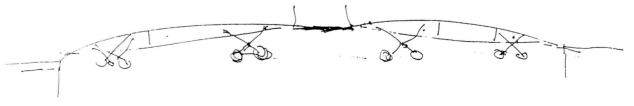

It's better to do architecture that is described as 'erotic' than to be labelled as 'high-tech' Amanda Levete

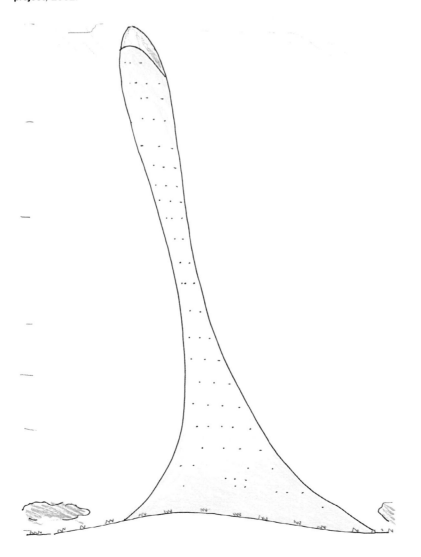

329 Biennale Tower, concept project, 2002.

f all the speculations that have marked Future Systems' evolution over the years, from their turbo-charged, high-tech beginnings, to their more recent interest in organic form as the point of departure for architecture, the one that has produced some of their most striking designs is also the one that so far remains the furthest from being realized. The ultra-tall tower has been a recurring theme in their work, which presents not just a technical challenge but an imaginative one too. Yet they have still not managed to build a skyscraper.

Future Systems have looked at innovative engineering solutions to extreme technical problems for clues pointing to new ways to build in less demanding circumstances. Unself-conscious engineering structures built for communications systems, or for the purposes of irrigation or defence, have been a continuing inspiration. But they have also explored the nature of ultra-high buildings as a conspicuous demonstration of their commitment to a particular view of what architecture can be. In Future Systems' hands, designing tall buildings is a reminder of the drive to use architecture to explore alternative and challenging visions of what life can be like. Their work on the high-rise has been based on an ambition to move away from the conventional, restricted mix of functions and spatial types that commonly characterize modern towers, and to offer a more dynamic interpretation of the potential of skyscrapers instead.

Despite the lingering hint of glamour attached to the skyscraper, with few exceptions, most tall buildings built so far have effectively been monocultures, devoted entirely to office space and empty for half the day, or else to residential use. At the same time, the drive for economy as a guiding principle in structural design has led to a high degree of repetition in layouts. Once the decision has been made between a concrete or a steel frame, for example, every floor is treated like every other one; only the entrance lobby, and sometimes the penthouse level, is allowed to deviate from the standard pattern. Often, structural grids have also had the effect of creating spatially bland and uniform interiors. These are constraints that have encouraged Future Systems to look for more radical interpretations of the typology of the high-rise. They have sought out forms that

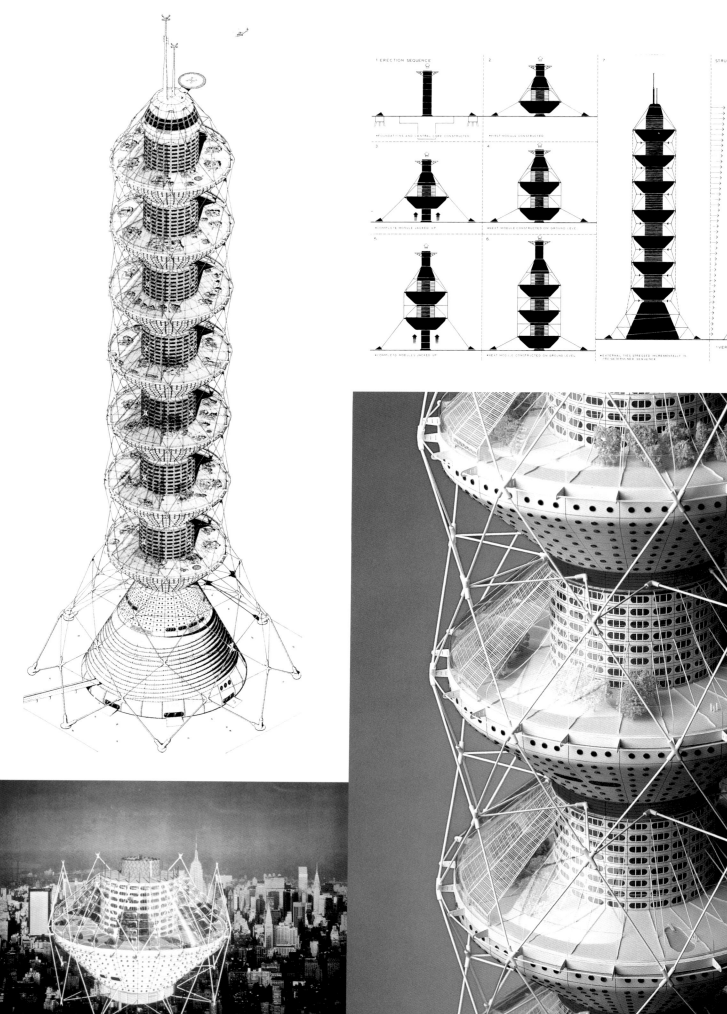

1 ERECTION SEQUENCE

STRUCTURAL SYSTEM

have the potential to offer a wider and richer range of spatial experiences and social purposes.

Their method has been to create new forms by pushing the high-rise type to extremes. They have deliberately attempted to design buildings beyond the limits of conventional constructional systems. With the memory of Buckminster Fuller in mind, they have considered creating single buildings on the scale of an entire town. Often, the idea of energy performance has been the catalyst for design concepts that move beyond the simple box and structural cage as the basis for building a tower. Future Systems have proposed incorporating wind turbines as integral elements of urban high-rises, and building circular cable-stayed towers of extreme height that incorporate external communal gardens at high level. Their designs for towers combine residential use with workspaces and recreation, in a mix that suggests some of the utopian projects of the 1920s. And beyond their work with engineering solutions, and their interest in the social and urban aspects of tall buildings, Future Systems have explored the formal possibilities, moving from their early, skeletal-exposed

112 Coexistence,
concept project, 1984.

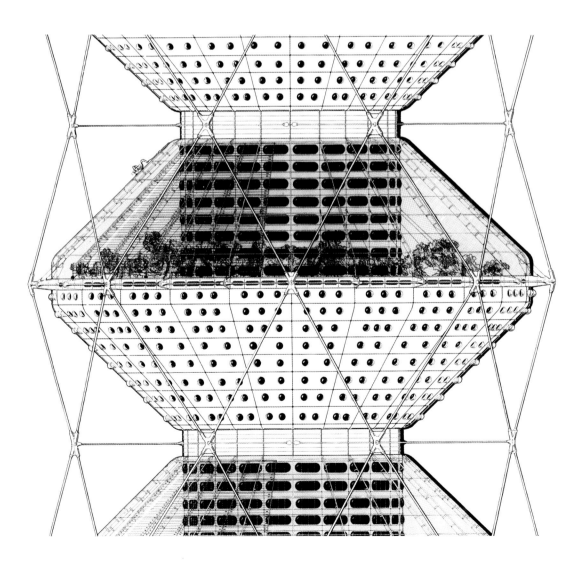

112
COEXISTENCE

GREEN BIRD

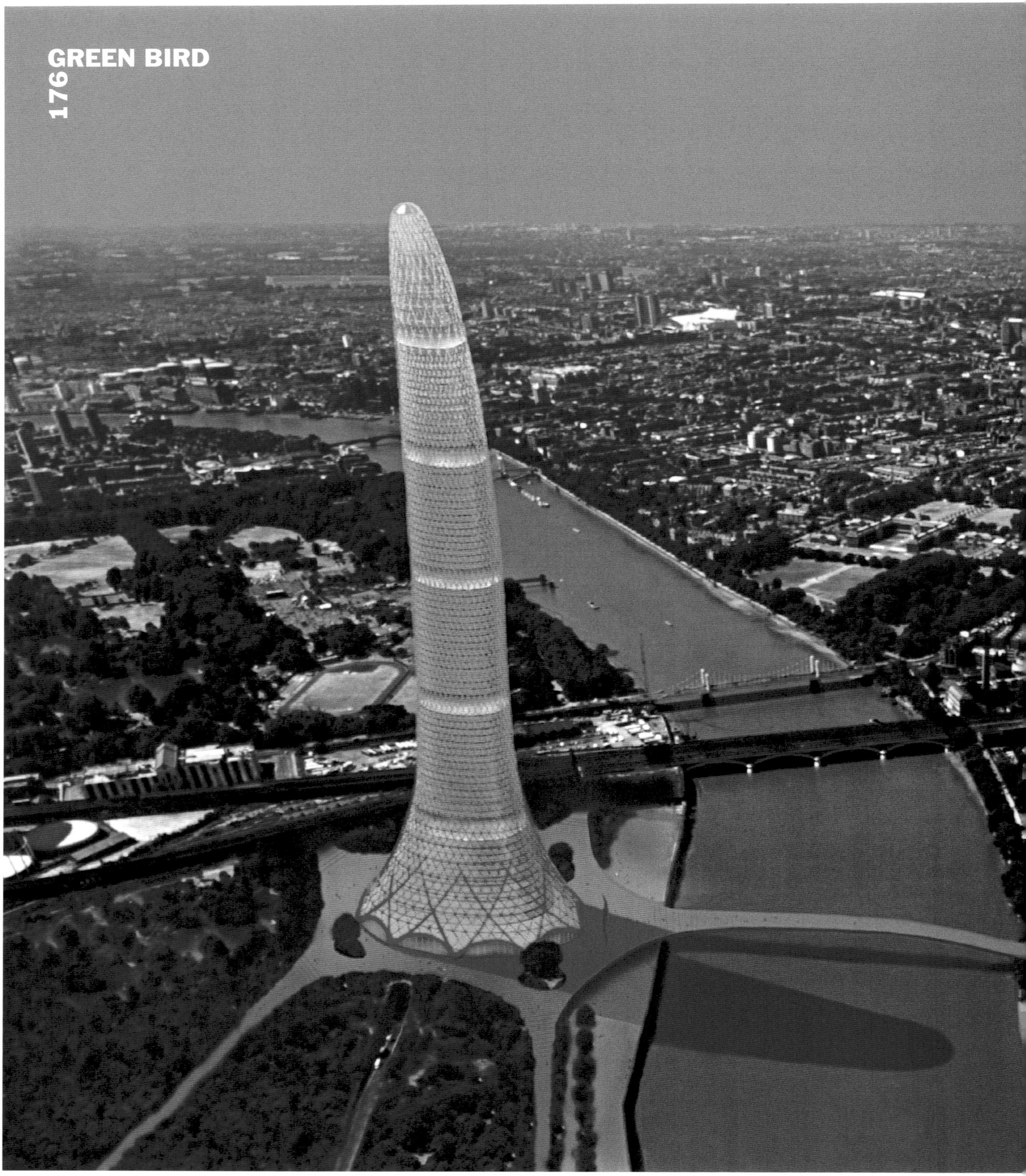

structures to complex curved surfaces that are only now becoming feasible.

It is not, of course, entirely outside the bounds of possibility that one of these towers, or something based fairly closely on it, will eventually be built. But in the absence of a developer or a construction company ready and able to take up their ideas of how the high-rise tower could be redefined, the prospect of a Future Systems-designed tallest building in the world is unlikely to be imminent. What is it then, that drives the firm to devote so much time and energy to speculating on the nature of tall buildings? Probably, it has something to do with the urge to explore what Levete and Kaplicky clearly believe is one of the fundamental architectural problems of modern times. If they do not engage with it, they cannot be fully part of the contemporary architectural discourse. And it is a reflection of their values and methods that they do not believe it necessary to build an idea for it to have an architectural impact. If the underlying vision is strong enough, and it is presented persuasively enough, then an architectural idea can be just as powerful as its physical realization. Mies van der Rohe's charcoal on yellow drafting paper studies for an undulating glass office tower, for example, constituted an utterly fantastic proposal in the context of Berlin in the 1920s. But they continued to haunt the architectural world's imagination until the multiple but flawed physical realizations of corporate modern glass boxes became an international commonplace in the 1960s. In their montages and their drawings, their Plasticine sketch models and their lovingly detailed larger models, as well as the engineering calculations prepared by their collaborators, Future Systems have created a series of propositions for the tower as it could be, rather than as it is.

As such, the studio has acted as a kind of open-access research laboratory, preparing prototypes and predictions that others have followed at a couple of removes. The question of originality in architecture, and even more of authorship, is a complex one, and ultimately not always the subject of fruitful debate. Architecture depends on many different inputs. Design is not an entirely autonomous process. And as Future Systems' extensive visual research shows with sharp clarity, there are many triggers and inspirations for new developments, in their case everything from nineteenth-century greenhouses and botanical specimens, to twentieth-century fortifications, fashion and aerospace technology. But Future Systems have certainly kept ahead of the curve in their ideas of what tall buildings can be, even if they have so far been unable to realize them for themselves. Their work has helped to make a redefinition of the tower possible.

One of the more memorable aspects of the Venice Architecture Biennale of 2002 was a cluster of large-scale models of skyscrapers, four metres high, produced especially for the show. The exhibition's opening took place exactly one year after the attacks on the twin towers of the World Trade Center and, as director of the Biennale, it seemed to me impossible not to acknowledge the magnitude of that event in some way, so I decided to address the ambivalence of the

176 Green Bird,
concept project, 1996.

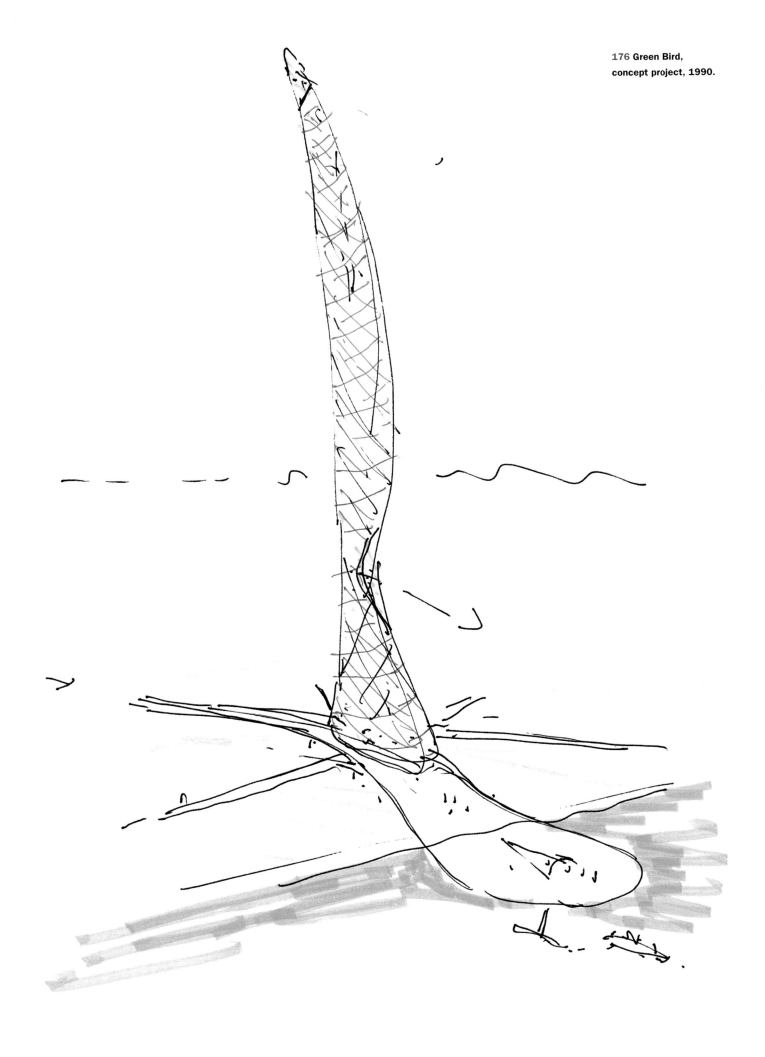

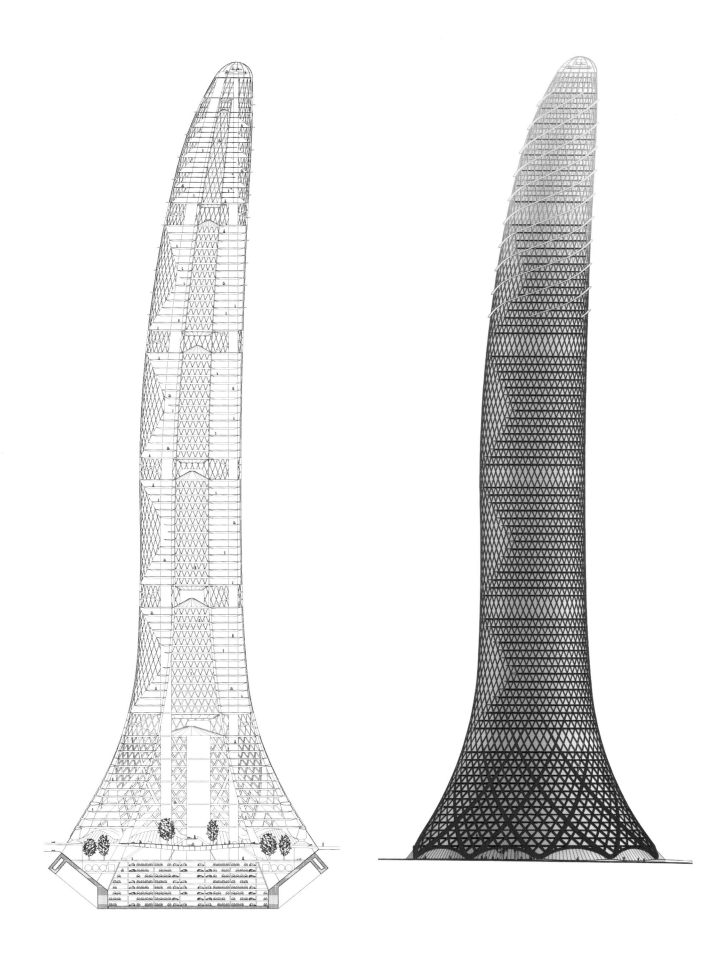

226 **ZED London,**
office building, 1995.

world of contemporary architecture in its attitudes to the ultra-high-rise tower.

It is a form that has alternately fascinated and repelled the world. The determination in the years leading up to 2001 to build ever-taller buildings, pushing further and further past the 100-floor barrier, could be seen as a reversion to a primitively obvious search for the most unsubtle symbols of potency and authority. And for a while, the idea of transforming the familiar skylines of the world's historic cities with conspicuous intrusions seemed to be diminishing them. Yet the renewed interest in these structures was often presented as a semi-utopian search for more urbane forms of city building, or as a way of achieving substantially higher densities than was feasible with any other building type, a quality seen as desirable in its reduction both of the consumption of

land and of the dependence on private transport. The tower could be understood as an essential underpinning for the culture of congestion represented by the Manhattan of the Rockefeller Center era, and the golden age of high-rise architecture in America from the Flat Iron to the Chrysler.

The collapse of the twin towers focused attention on the symbolic meaning of all very tall buildings, as well as the technical issues of their safety, and their occupants' need for psychological reassurance. Briefly, it even seemed possible that the future of high-rise itself was in doubt. A twisted, buckled piece of steel from Yamasaki's twin towers lay on the ground outside the American Pavilion in Venice, along with a series of speculations about the redevelopment of the site. To address the question of the future of the high-rise from a more oblique view, I invited a group of architects – some of whom had built tall structures, most of whom had not – to speculate from a range of different theoretical viewpoints on the design of an ultra-tall tower that would push through the 100-floor limit. The group included Jean Nouvel, Toyo Ito, David Chipperfield and Zaha Hadid, as well as Future Systems.

I remember walking into the space devoted to the installation – a seventeenth-century rope works in Venice's Arsenale – just before the exhibition opened, to see the last of the tower models being brought in. It happened to be Future Systems' polished stainless-steel vision of a leaning tower with a rounded tip, pierced by an almond-shaped opening. It was being brought in on lifting tackle, and looked a lot like a battering ram. Hoisted up into position at eye level, it was the most militantly

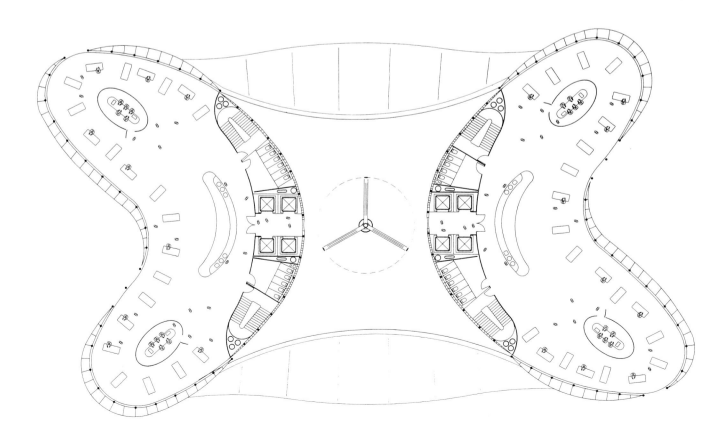

365 **Berlin Alexanderplatz,**
department store and office
building, 2003.

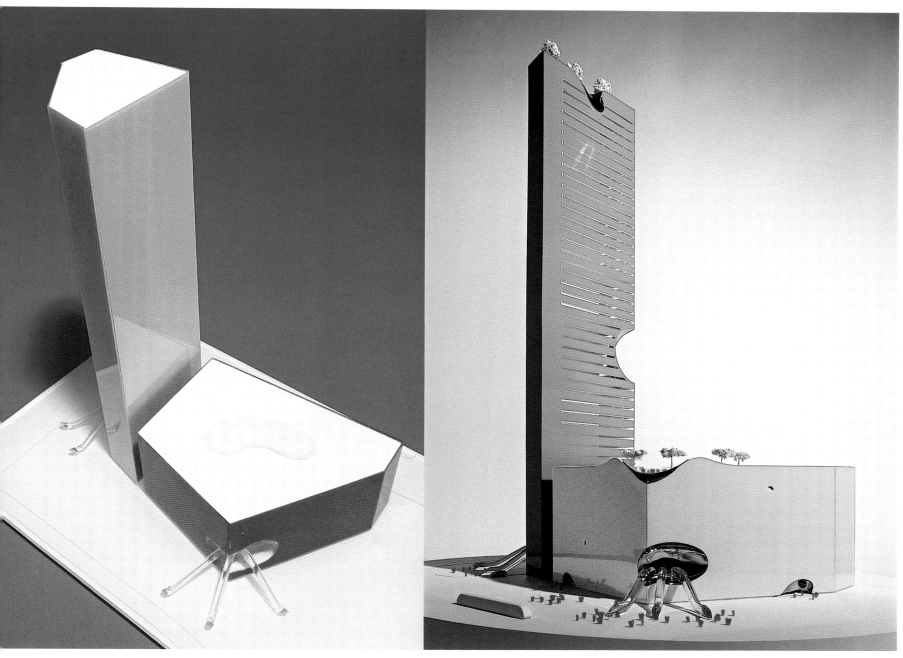

phallic of all the schemes, the most uncomfortable, the most vulnerable in its frankness, and in its readiness to take aesthetic risks that put it quite outside the normal architectural comfort zone.

The design has as much to say about the nature of Future Systems' attitude to architecture and design as it does about tall buildings. It is a reflection of what can look at times like naivety and artlessness, but turns out more often to be bravery in their work. Future Systems are ready to put themselves well out in front of the architectural pack, without turning round to see what is happening behind them before adopting a new direction, or taking into account the possible response to their lack of caution. With the leaning tower, Future Systems were moving beyond the alibi of structural determinism, or historical precedent, and proposing a new architectural language for ultra-tall buildings, which others have subsequently taken up.

Future Systems have found the confidence to pursue sculptural ends with such speculations, looking for inspiration in organic forms, but their work is still

tempered by a grasp of structural imperatives. In the end, their design for Venice, with its spreading base, its tapering shaft and its pierced top, did follow the dictates of skyscraper building logic in terms of wind resistance and resistance to turning moments. Even the idea of a tilted lift shaft, like an ultra-steep funicular cable car, implied as a requirement for the project, was something that Rem Koolhaas was thinking about at almost exactly the same moment, with what was still a secret competition submission for the new Central China television headquarters.

In the relatively short history of the skyscraper, developments have come in sudden leaps, interspersed by periods of relative stability. The solutions adopted for structural stability have tended to be targeted at specific heights. Breaking through each successive limit has required the formulation of new conceptual models to deal with them, which have had the effect of creating new archetypes for tower forms. The optimum form for a tower of around forty storeys is different from that of an eighty-floor structure. Varying sets of problems are posed in each case. Wind resistance, as opposed to dead weight, becomes more significant in taller towers, and requires different formal and structural solutions. And new economic calculations come into play for taller towers when an increasing percentage of the floor area is eaten up by the lift cores required to service the upper levels. Such considerations have had the effect not just of encouraging the exploration of alternative bracing systems, but have also resulted in designs that have avoided flat tops for towers, since narrower tops reduce wind load.

At the heart of much speculation about the nature of the high-rise is the idea of introducing new kinds of circulation routes within such buildings, as well as new combinations of types of space, rather than the straightforward repetition of the cellular structure of most column-and-beam towers, stabilized by their cores. The earliest towers used historical precedents to create an architectural language that suggested a sense of stylistic continuity in order to domesticate the unfamiliarity of ultra-tall buildings. Mies van der Rohe formulated a new language for the tower, revealing the structural logic of a frame-and-skin construction. The immateriality of glass turned out to be both a liberation and a trap, since it created a conceptual straightjacket of crystalline forms, and in the end ran counter to the demands of tailoring high-rise structures to deal with the question of energy performance. It was to be a point of departure for Future Systems' work with the engineers at Arup, specializing in formulating innovative ways of dealing with highly serviced buildings.

The Venice installation came at a moment when the skyscraper was on the edge of making a paradigm shift. The conventional tripartite formula of base-plus-shaft-plus-top for its aesthetic treatment was about to be displaced by attempts to reconfigure the type following the idea of a vertical extrusion of a city instead of single, isolated, tall buildings. Many of the submissions for the Ground Zero competition the following year looked in this direction, and were based on linked clusters of towers, with complex internal circulation patterns. Clearly, the nature of the high-rise as a building type was already fluid and ready for some radical new thinking.

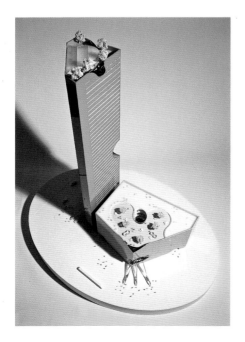

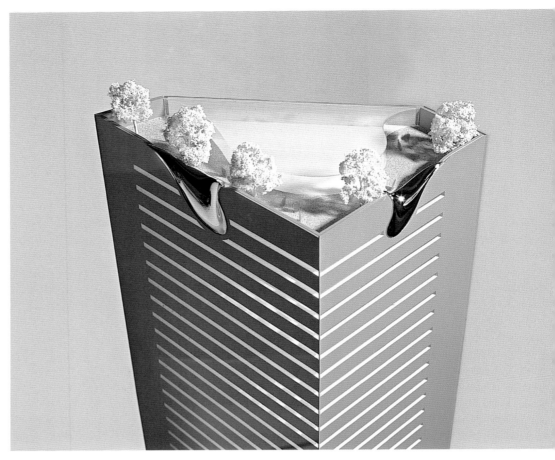

The Venice project was not Future Systems' first attempt at engaging with this kind of material. Two decades earlier, they had speculated about a giant skyscraper, with a circular plan, braced by an external series of stacked volumes. David Nixon, Kaplicky's partner at the time, called it a response to the rapid urbanization of the majority of the world. Designed in 1984 with a non-specific urban site in mind, the Coexistence tower would have had 150 floors, containing almost 700 apartments, and approaching three million square feet of office space. It could have accommodated as many as 10,000 people at any one time, and took the form of a stack of seven climate-controlled bubbles, with a circular structural and service core running through its centre and an outer geodesic structural web. Kaplicky had worked for Norman Foster on the submission for the Hong Kong and Shanghai Bank tower, and there are perhaps echoes of its hanging tiers of offices floors, as well as its externally expressed complex structure. It adopted the cantilevered, disc-shaped helicopter landing pad, and the twin communications masts as spires that were the distinguishing features of many towers designed at that time. And in its spider's-web steel structure – which seemed to owe something to the Eastern European tradition of extreme engineering, using a minimum of mass to create strength, together with a multiplicity of members – it reflected the design that Future Systems had submitted for the competition to build a landmark in Melbourne a couple of years previously.

By the time Future Systems produced their next speculative high-rise, the Green Bird tower in 1990, they were moving in what looked like a rather different direction, though one that the Foster team would soon

365 **Berlin Alexanderplatz, department store and office building, 2003.**

follow. The tower's thrusting form and curved plan gave it as unmistakably phallic a silhouette as has ever been seriously contemplated for a skyscraper. This reading is particularly evident in the presentation of the project in model form. The pink colour and the shape irresistibly suggest a sexual interpretation. Levete remembers her initial reaction as she saw the nearly completed model:

> When I first saw the Green Bird, I was stunned. I hadn't understood that it could be seen as so overt. We talked about using colour to give it a different, less literal quality. I asked for the spirals to be finished in a really intense colour. At first I found the phallic interpretation embarrassing, but I realized that it's better to do architecture that's described as 'erotic' than labelled as 'high-tech'. Since the Green Bird, there has been the Swiss Re tower and Jean Nouvel's equally explicit Torre Agbar in Barcelona, and the project has lost something of the initial sense of shock.

That Future Systems are far from rejecting sensuality as an architectural image can be seen in the way in which the undulating skin of the Selfridges store is penetrated by its bridge. But as suggested by the popularity of the Swiss Re tower, designed five years later by Norman Foster and his team, these references are transformed in their nature by the jump in scale to a full-sized building. The initial strangeness, even its shocking quality, is dissipated by familiarity once it becomes a fixed part of the skyline and it begins to take on other, more abstract, associations. It is remarkable how quickly the transgressive can become the routine background to everyday life.

For Kaplicky, the negative response to the Green Bird from those who could see it only as a phallic symbol was simply inexplicable. Levete explains the practice's approach to criticism:

> We don't protect ourselves with theory. For us, architecture is a way of thinking, it's inside your skin. Some people learn from the plan; for me architecture is more about feeling and emotional responses and understanding. I've never been a great talker about the plan or the section. It's what a building feels like

to touch, how you walk into a space, and its impact and how your mood changes that matters for me. I enjoy and judge and experience buildings as a matter of proportion and light. That leaves you very emotionally exposed when you're proposing something new. At the beginning, Jan and I always described the work in technological ways, as if it were the only solution. I suppose that suggests a lack of confidence. People's reactions would start from a sense of incredulity, so we'd talk about the work in technical terms of the most efficient structure. But it wasn't about that, and in the last five years we've both felt able to be less inhibited and talk about what we do in a more subjective way.

The point of the Green Bird project was not primarily to introduce sexually explicit imagery into architecture. It was more a determination to harness the form of a tall building to act as a benign climate modifier and energy generator, and to explore a new structural system for a very tall tower. The Green Bird, like Jean Nouvel's unbuilt Tour Sans Fin for Paris, would have had a void at its centre, in place of the usual structural core, depending on asymmetrically placed stair and lift towers and the diagonal bracing of its structural grid for stability. And it was a similar idea that drove the design of Future Systems' tower for Venice. On a smaller scale, their work on Project ZED (1995) – a research exercise in combining high-density housing with self-sufficiency in energy generation – also used the form of the building to generate energy, incorporating a wind turbine within the envelope of a pair of residential towers, clustered together as a twin block.

In 2003, after the success of the Selfridges building in Birmingham, Future Systems were asked to work on a proposal for a city-centre store in Berlin that would have formed the base for an office tower. The budget, and the context, did not allow for anything on the lines of their earlier experiments, but their schematic design demonstrated an inventive subversion of the conventional parameters, with minimal interventions in the skin of the tall block, and a dialogue between low and tall, suggesting how a Future Systems tower might actually come to be realized.

The design was a response to an enquiry from the American development company Hines, who were looking for a bold strategy for a tall tower with a department store at its base for a site in the former East Berlin, on the edge of the Socialist Realist slice of the city, close to the Alexanderplatz. Kaplicky responded with relish to the challenge, proposing a strong injection of colour, with green, yellow and pink, and even introducing strongly organic forms, within the constraints of a cost-effective rectangular envelope, by gouging holes out of the box, like giant honeycomb bubbles, which played against the rectilinear forms. In common with Selfridges, a key element would have been the centre's closely integrated parking.

Another attempt to tailor their research to the demands of the marketplace was Future Systems' unsuccessful proposal for a mid-rise residential tower in Manhattan. The project, for a site on Broadway, would have occupied a site too narrow for more than a handful of apartments on each floor. Undulating balconies would have distinguished its facade. It was an application of the kind of inventiveness that informs all Future Systems' work, and put their knowledge gained from thinking about the problems of building high-rises to use at a variety of scales: high-rise, mid-rise and low-rise.

The kind of thinking about material qualities and tactility generated by the collaboration with Anthony Gormley on the Wembley project can be seen in other examples of their work, even in such an apparently unpromising project as a low-budget commission to modernize a bland 1960s office building just off London's Oxford Street. The problem here is that space is strictly limited, and the building is on a narrow street and is very overlooked. The strategy was to reskin the building with a material that Levete compares to a tightly stretched rubber skirt. What looks like a series of slits, like those in a Lucio Fontana canvas, accommodate strip windows that bring overhead sunlight into the interior. So limited is the space inside that there is no room for a ground-floor reception area. Instead, a lift takes visitors straight up to a double-height space on the top storey. The walls will be made of a special rubber silica with a glassy, reflective surface, which is used for car parks but has never been deployed vertically before. The base of the building will be a stainless-steel ribbon. And out of this unpromising material, Future Systems will have made an object with undoubtedly sculptural qualities, even if it remains a piece of architecture.

Against a background in which every ambitious city from Shanghai to Dubai is frantically trying to build ever-more flamboyant and exotic towers, and even London's skyline is experiencing a period of violent transition, Future Systems' interest in the high-rise is timely. They have played an under-acknowledged part in shifting perceptions of what is possible in this field.

388 Hills Place, office building, London, 2004.

135 Blob, office building,
London, 1985.

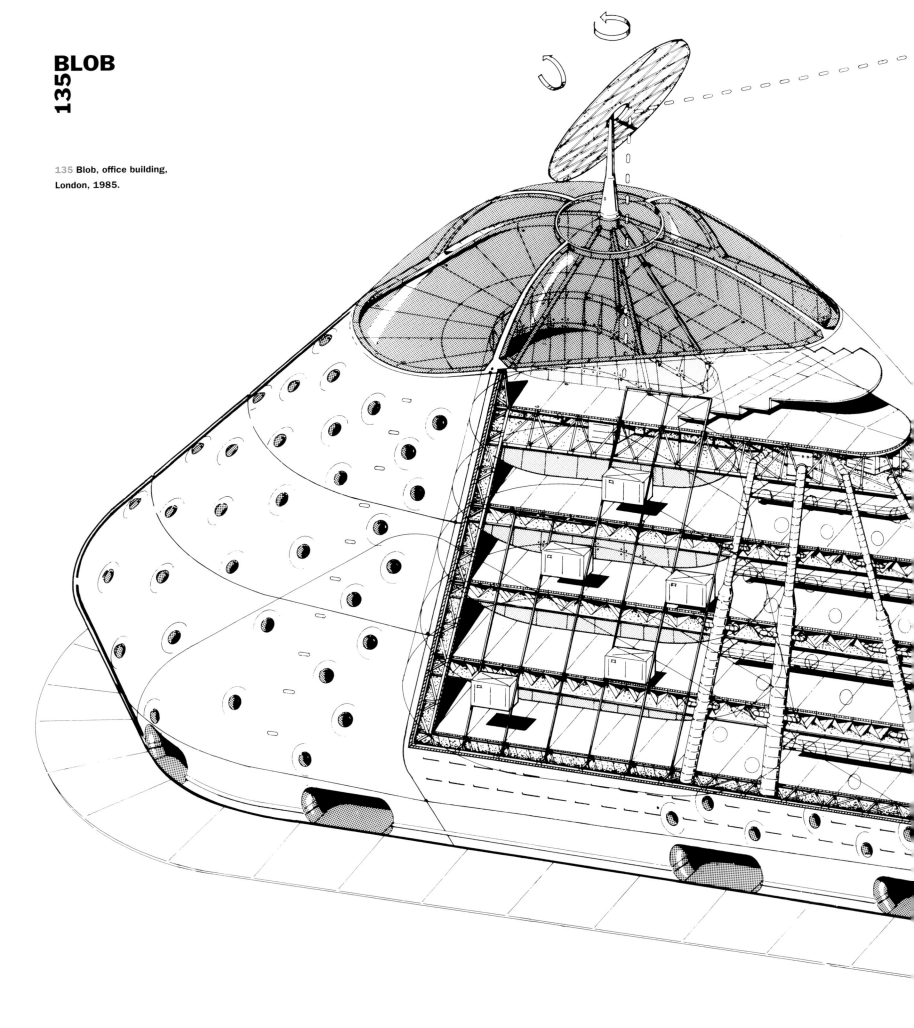

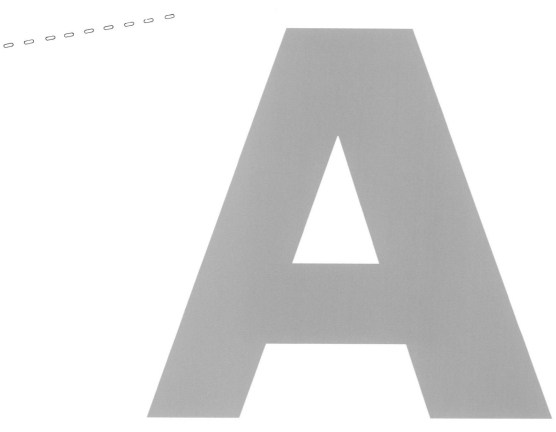

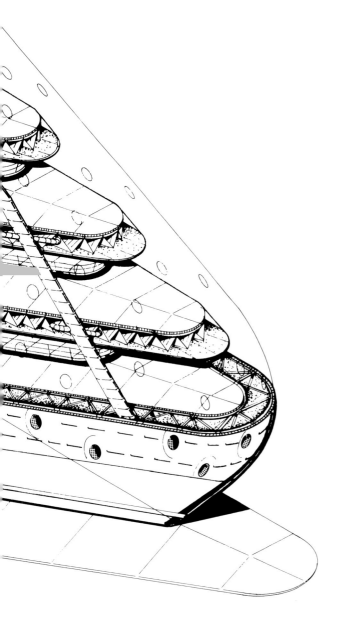

A

fter thirty years in which neutrality and aesthetic restraint were prized as aesthetic virtues, the landmark has re-emerged over the last decade as an abiding preoccupation for a significant sector of the architectural community. Forty years ago, Buckminster Fuller's domes were a unique one-off, as were the shells of Jørn Utzon's submission for the Sydney Opera House competition, though they were arresting enough to persuade one of the jurors to attempt something similarly dramatic in his design for the TWA terminal at John F Kennedy Airport in New York. But despite the seductive appeal of these isolated examples, there remained a certain suspicion of such energetic invention, especially among those who saw what they understood to be the rationalism of modernity as incompatible with the rhetoric of the form-makers.

Those reservations have evaporated, and a search for new geometries has percolated every corner of the architectural world, producing a wave of folded plates, complex curves and fractals. The phenomenon is more than the result of a burst of *fin-de-siècle* exuberance; it is the product of a diverse range of factors that stretch all the way from a hunger for richer, more powerful forms of architectural expression to the escalating reduction in the cost of computing power that has made it possible seriously to pursue alternatives to traditional orthogonal geometry on the building site.

The competition between ambitious provincial cities for international tourism and investment is also a factor, as is the development of new building technologies that make customized, complex skins possible at a reasonable cost. It is a development that has rendered architecture a much more visible part of the cultural landscape, engaging a wider audience than it has ever previously enjoyed. But at its most negative, it is a preoccupation that has at times threatened to reduce architecture to the production of sensational and superficial spectacle, to be used as backdrop in car advertisements.

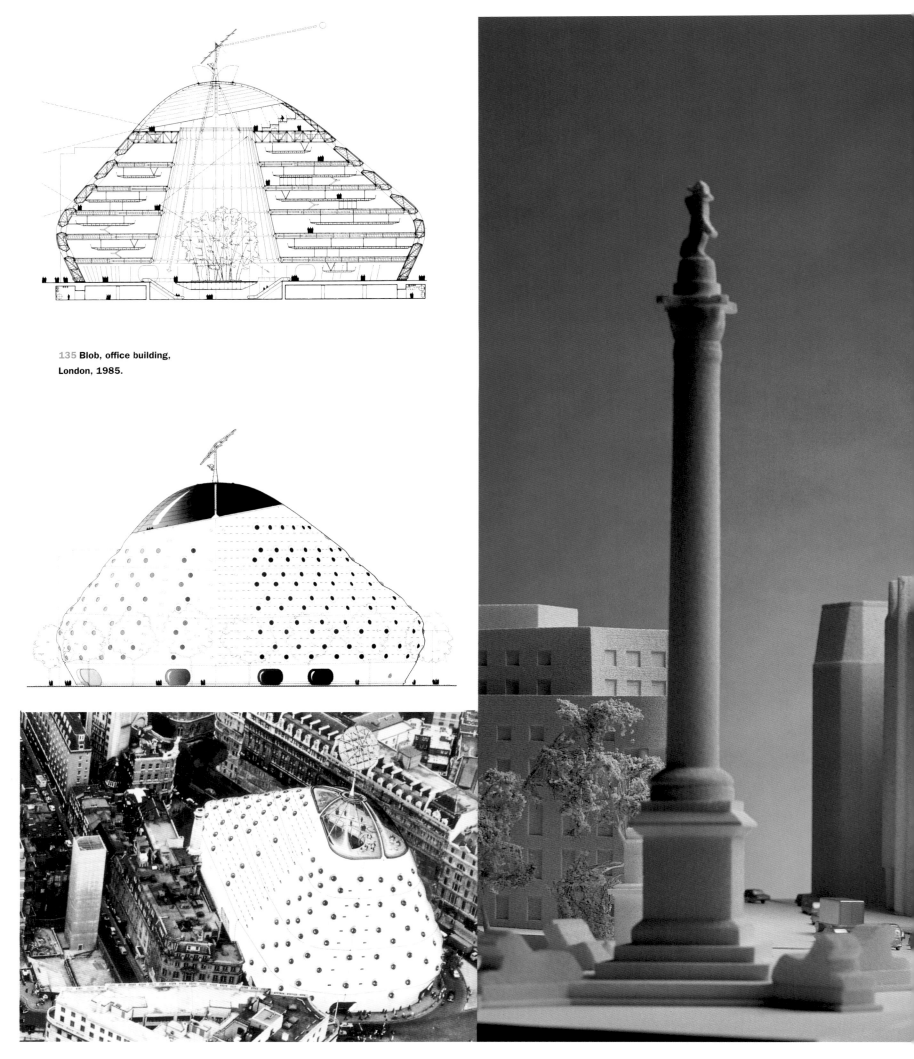

135 **Blob, office building,**
London, 1985.

More constructively, it has made possible a series of striking new buildings that feed off each other in their inventiveness. It is a phenomenon that might be seen as reflecting a search for an alternative to the banality of so much contemporary architectural production. For Future Systems, who have certainly played a significant and highly visible part in this shift, it is an expression of a restless determination to go on looking for new directions, a reluctance to accept the status quo and a continuing search for new ways to energize design.

Future Systems' research has seen its focus move from an early preoccupation with the aesthetic possibilities of aerospace and aeronautical engineering, prefabrication and technology transfer, following in the footsteps of Charles Eames, towards a more fluid exploration of shape and natural form that acknowledges Oscar Niemeyer and Erich Mendelsohn among other inspirations. And, most recently, they have begun to practice a more autonomous form of architecture, edging away from pragmatic constraint towards emotional expression and art.

Future Systems' work has both helped to shape a new sensibility, and been shaped by a climate in which a range of architects from Frank Gehry to Zaha Hadid have looked for new design languages. In contrast to the roughness of Gehry's work, achieved through a continual, painterly journey of discovery, or the more crystalline approach of Hadid, Future Systems' work is based on a kind of intuitive search for formal perfection. Their designs seek to create complete worlds that have their own internal logic and consistency, and which can step outside the mundane, as well as avoiding the conventional flaws and compromises of the building process, but somehow still also manage to maintain a foothold in pragmatic construction.

It took almost fifteen years for Kaplicky's first speculations on a new formal geometry to be realized. The major step in his development from his identity before the mid-1980s as the personification of turbo-charged high-tech was the scheme he submitted in 1985 for the competition for Grand Buildings, a prominent but redundant Edwardian structure on the south side of Trafalgar Square in London. This was a point of departure in several ways. Kaplicky had recently left Norman Foster's studio and Future Systems had become his exclusive creative outlet. The competition design was an effective way of announcing that step publicly and distancing himself from his past. But it also marked a transition in his own thinking, away from his earlier preoccupation with the imagery of the machine, and a move towards more organic forms.

Trafalgar Square, it should be remembered, was the great battleground of British architecture in the 1980s. It was the National Gallery's attempts to build a new extension on the north-west corner of the square that had attracted the fury of the Prince of Wales and triggered his notorious 'carbuncle' speech the previous year. The entire purpose of the competition was to provide the developers staging it with an escape hatch from an impossible problem. On the opposite corner of the square, they had a building that was worthless to them

because it could not be adapted to meet the demands of any conceivable contemporary users who could afford the rent demanded by its extraordinarily prominent site, but nor could they persuade the planning authorities to let them demolish it. The competition was intended to produce a commercially viable design for a new building with predominantly office use that would satisfy the planners and the heritage lobby, and at the same time fend off a rampant prince bent on saving the world from any more conspicuously contemporary architecture. Future Systems' entry was shockingly, even perversely, different from every other submission. In the circumstances, it is not surprising that it got nowhere in a competition eventually won by a feeble scheme to reconstruct a replica of the existing facade in stone to conceal a new interior. That proposal, whose very banality made some take it to be a nuanced piece of avante-gardism rather than expediency, was duly built.

On one level, Future Systems' design was suicidally brave, a riposte to the received wisdom of the time about contextualism. But it did point to the new directions that the practice would continue to explore and eventually to build. With an innovative structure that would have suspended a stack of office floors from a portal frame, the building took the form of a hollowed-out blob, its central atrium lit through sunlight collected by a roof-top array of mirrors, and clad in a white ceramic skin. It constituted a new direction for Kaplicky, and its shape was a marker that others have moved to follow over the years. Looking back, it could be said that Future Systems' blob did have its contextual aspects. Its swooping curves followed the precedent set by the original Grand Buildings, with its grandiloquent stone facades. In terms of its colour and mass, if not in its detail or its form, the blob offered a viable alternative to the conventional approach to building in a historic context. And its relatively quiet means of expression was clearly adopted in deference to the National Gallery, which dominates Trafalgar Square from the north side, opposite. Nor was this going to be an all-glass structure; the skin might have been doubly curved, but it clearly looked like a wall, punctured by windows. Kaplicky conceived these as circular portholes, believing that adopting a form curved in section and plan meant that the openings in that form would have to accept the curve as well, and not fight against it with straight lines and right angles.

For Future Systems to move from the speculative imaginative leap of the Grand Buildings competition to

171 **Bibliothèque de France, library, Paris, 1989.**

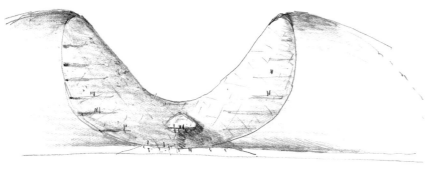

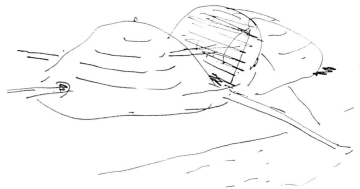

the confident assurance of Selfridges department store in Birmingham took a series of steps. Perhaps the most crucial was Levete's decision to join the practice in time for the French national library competition in 1989, which they came tantalizingly close to winning. Levete was determined to build, and had drive and ambition, as well as her own aesthetic perspective. Future Systems' work became more fluid and sculptural with her arrival.

The library was a landmark project in every sense. The site on the eastern fringes of central Paris was deliberately chosen to demonstrate that a national institution could serve to transform a bleak area deprived of the energy and life of the city centre. The library was also seen as a means of signalling the prestige of the French state, and its commitment to architectural innovation in its national landmarks. Finally, it was a personal monument to Mitterrand and his Pharonic view of the French political system, and the president even speeded up the project so that he could inaugurate it before his death.

The international jury, which included IM Pei and Richard Rogers, selected Future Systems submission as one of two schemes to recommend to President Mitterrand, leaving him to make a final decision for himself. Perhaps not entirely surprisingly, he followed his predilection for Cartesian geometry and opted for Dominique Perrault and his four identical glass towers.

When you **design** a **simple** object **over a** complex form, unexpected things happen. But **it's better** than you could have **imagined** Amanda Levete

221 Lords Media Centre, Marylebone Cricket Club, London, 1994.

221 Lords Media Centre, Marylebone Cricket Club, London, 1994.

Future Systems' idea had been to build a library that was designed for people and books, rather than electronic systems. It was a library that was intended to be popular and accessible. Their submission was the only one that proposed the incorporation of a pedestrian bridge to connect the remote Seine-side site with the other bank of the river. The library itself took the form of a partly hollowed-out glass mountain with a valley cut out of its heart to make way for the footbridge, offering passers-by a glimpse into its innermost workings and at the same time giving readers a sense that they were not entirely disconnected from the outside world. The curvaceous form meant that Future Systems had among the smallest

of the footprints of all the submissions, in part because their design allowed for the provision of additional storage space below ground.

If Future Systems had won the library competition, it would have swept the practice at one stroke into the premier league. But it would have been a far from easy transition, one that would have put Kaplicky and Levete under huge pressure. Instead, they moved forward by more gradual steps. Ever since Michael Hopkins built the new stands for Lords cricket ground, the Marylebone Cricket Club had become one of Britain's more unlikely patrons of contemporary architecture. Over the years, the guardians of traditional cricket commissioned not

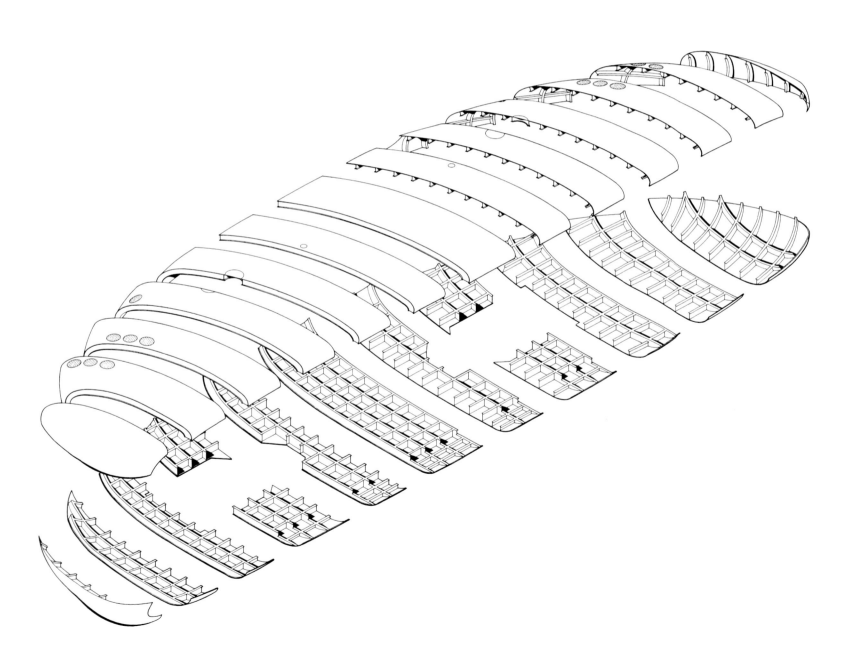

just Hopkins, but David Morley, who designed a practice complex, and then Future Systems to build a Media Centre to accommodate all the journalists from both television and print media who cover an international test match. In 1994, Peter Bell, an architect member of the Lords Committee, came to Future Systems in search of some lateral thinking. He had a problem with sight screens, and the gap between two stands that he wanted to use for more seats. Finally, Lords staged a competition for the press box.

Future Systems won, with a radical proposal for a glass-fronted white aluminium disc, raised up on two legs to project out on top of the stands. It was designed

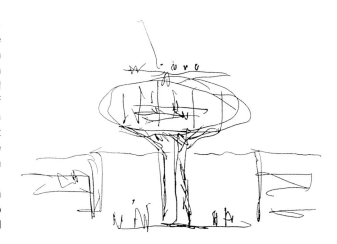

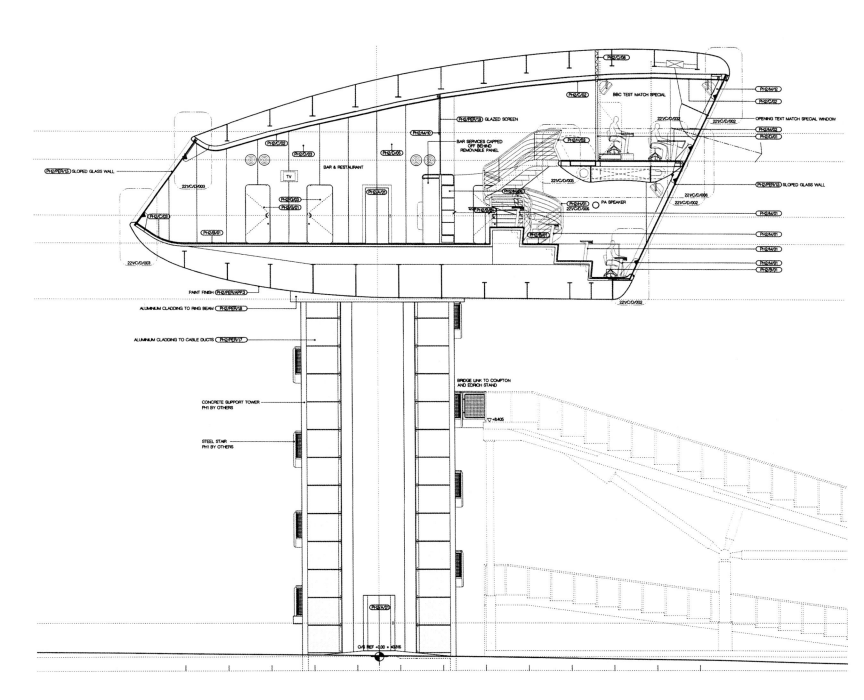

so that it could be built outside the cricket season without disruption to the game. What began as a purely technical problem became a chance for Kaplicky to realize the idea of a large-scale monocoque structure. For the first time, he was able to bring the practice of the boat-building industry to the construction site, to realize the synthesis of shell and structure that had obsessed him for so long. Though its scale is relatively modest, the Media Centre remains one of Future Systems' most ambitious projects – the ultimate realization of the semi-monocoque dream that Kaplicky has pursued for so long, a seamless aluminium structure.

Nothing on the same scale had been attempted before. There was no formula available for testing aluminium's performance under the provisions of the building regulations, and the techniques needed to produce members capable of handling structural loads were unfamiliar to the construction industry. It was too big to make out of GRP, which in any case is an unpleasant and laborious process. And Future Systems were determined to use aluminium, conceptually a much more elegant material. Kaplicky and Levete toured the Boat Show in search of boat builders skilled in making aluminium hulls. They discovered Pendennis, a Falmouth-based shipbuilding company that was more confident about taking on the project than any of the conventional construction companies that they approached to tender for the job. The Media Centre's ribs and spars were made exactly like those of an aluminium-hulled boat. Each was cut and bent specially to fit, but the process was made more difficult by the fact that the first design drawings were done by hand. It was only when the

221 Lords Media Centre, Marylebone Cricket Club, London, 1994.

We realized from the first site visit, and looking at the view from the Rotunda, that there was the need for a building here that had the potential to be a landmark

Jan Kaplicky

SELFRIDGES
BIRMINGHAM 279

279 **Selfridges Birmingham,** department store, 1999.

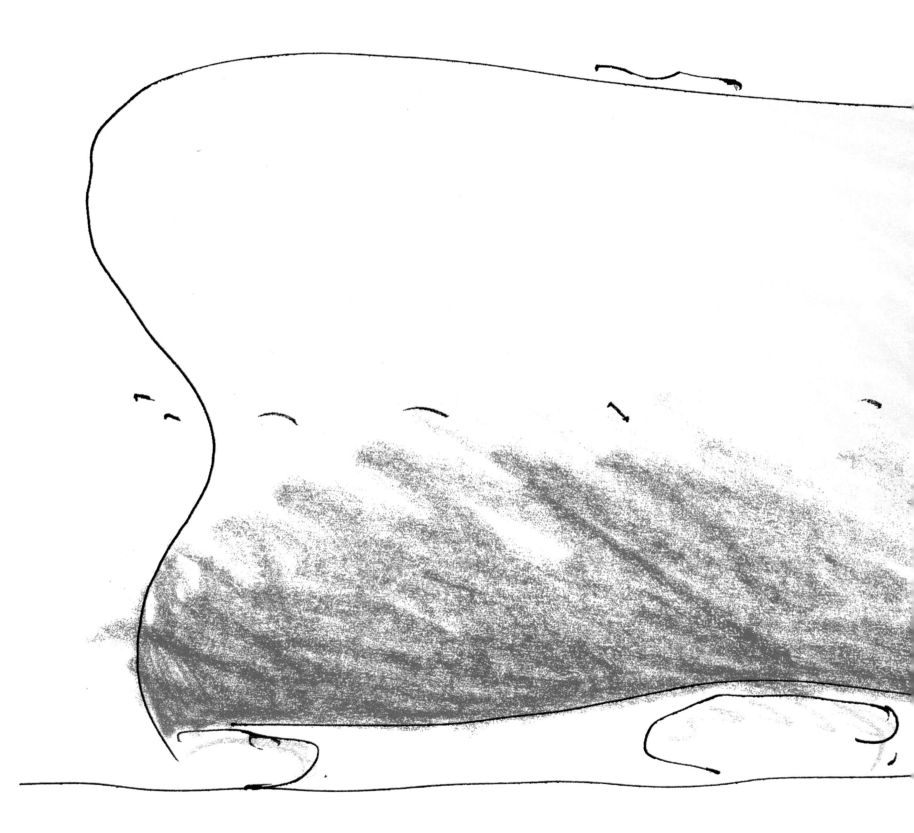

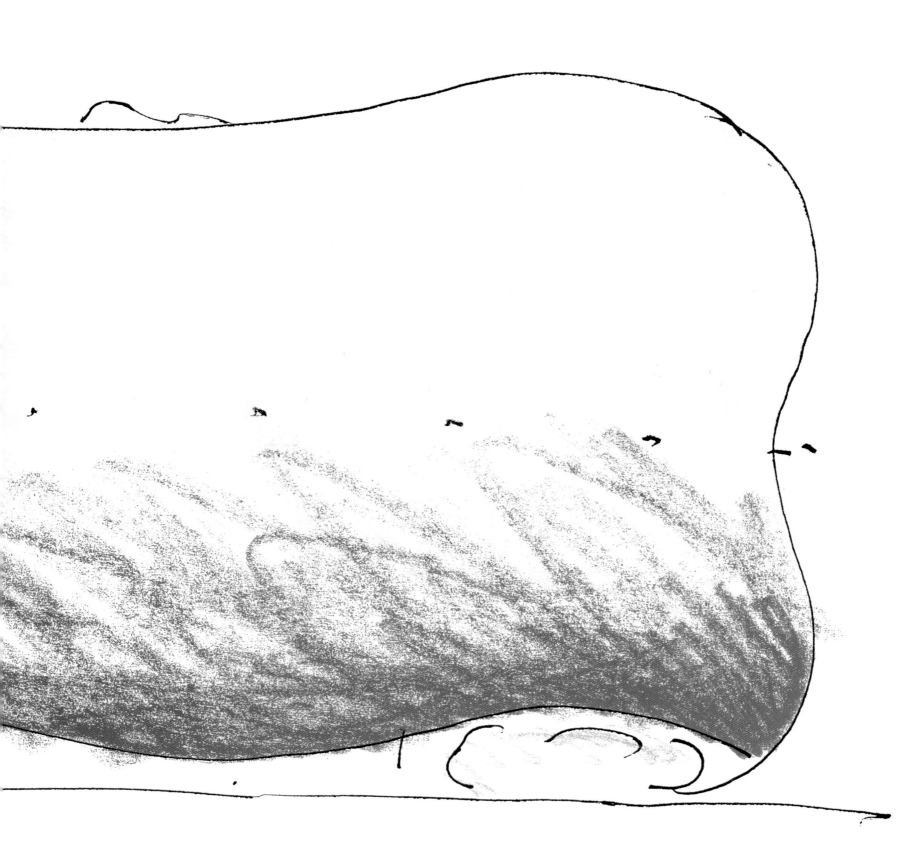

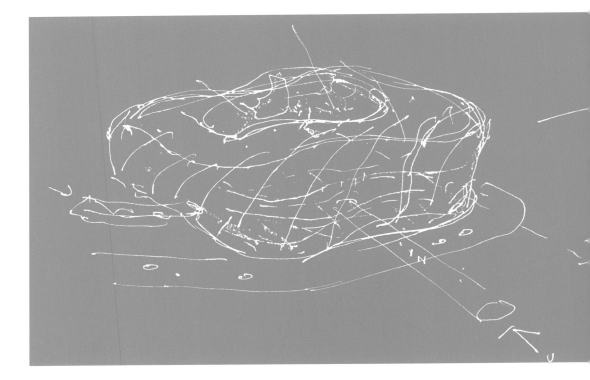

279 Selfridges Birmingham,
department store, 1999.

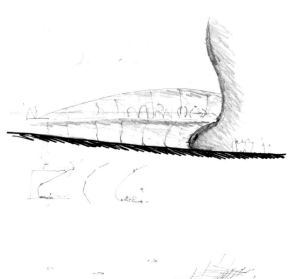

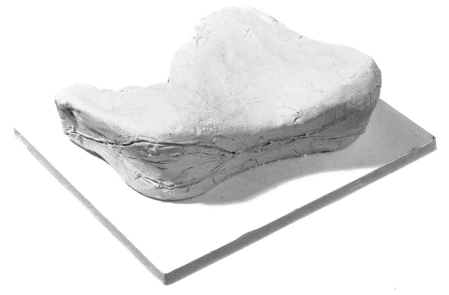

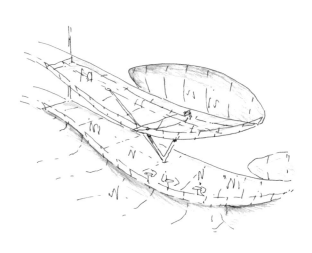

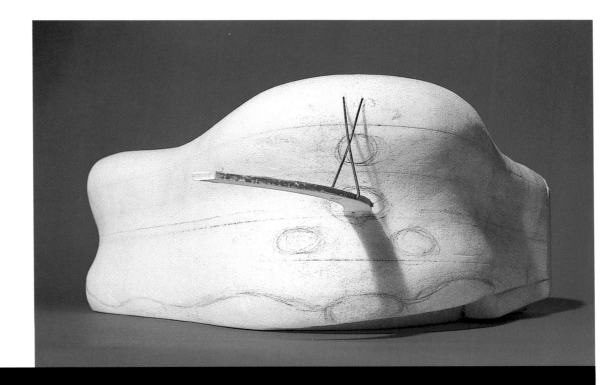

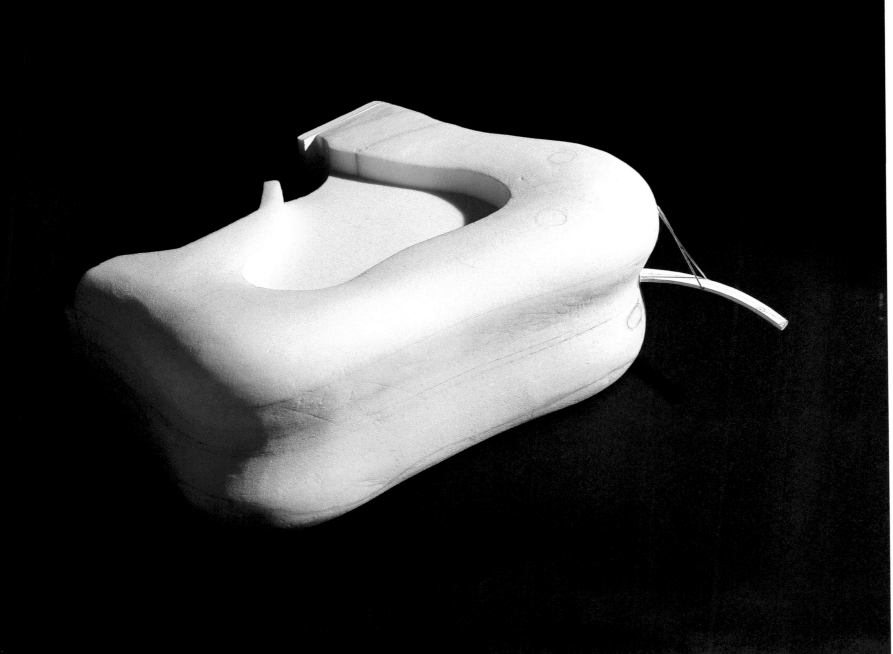

SMALLBROOK QUEENSWAY

DEBENHAMS

BULLRING BIRM

PERSHORE STREET

GLOUCESTER STREET

EDGBASTON STREET

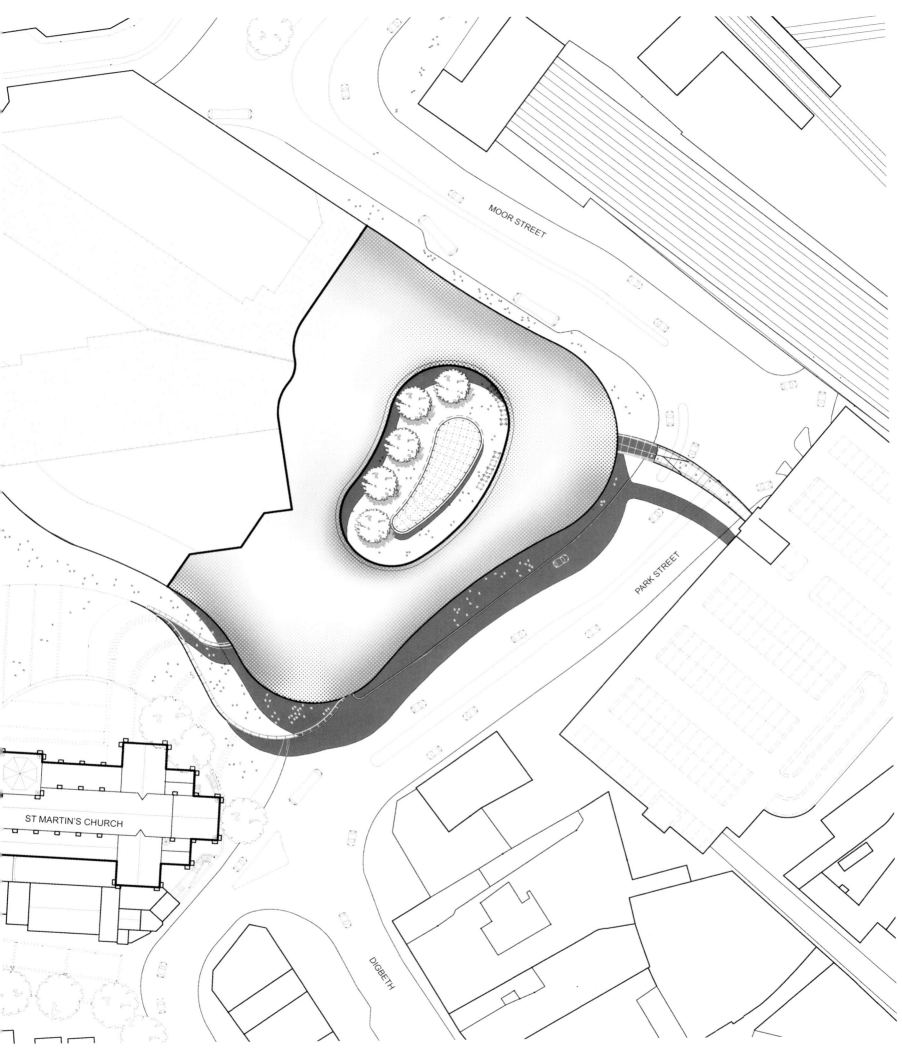

MOOR STREET

PARK STREET

ST MARTIN'S CHURCH

DIGBETH

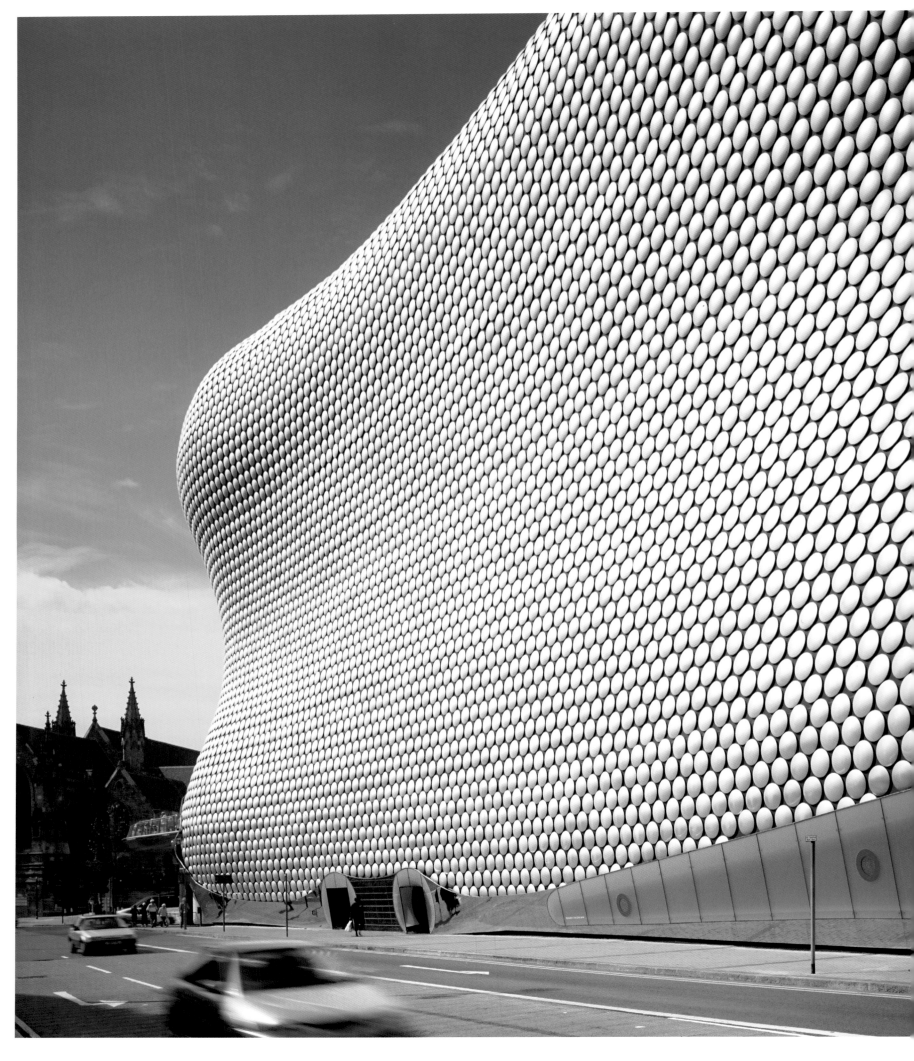

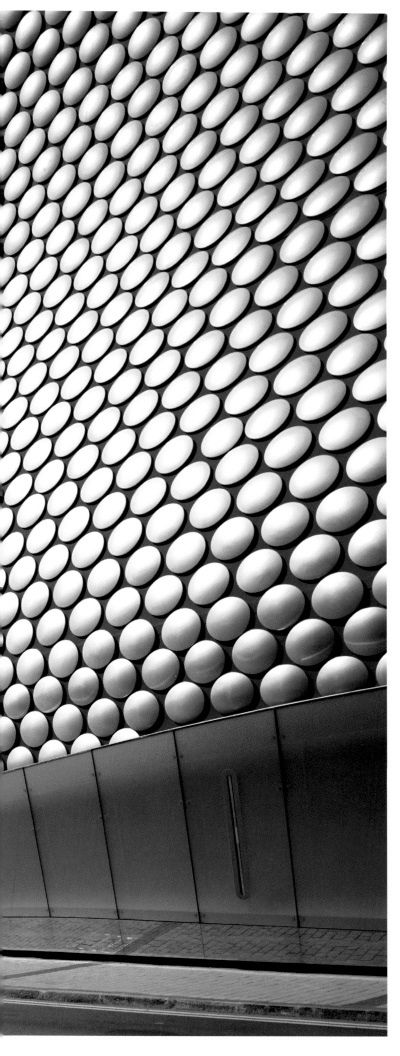

process was well underway that Future Systems finally embraced the computer.

Pendennis knew what it was doing with structural aluminium, but it was used to building boats upside down in its yard. For the Media Centre, it had to bring its workforce to London, and dry-assemble and weld the components in situ.

Installation was not as smooth as Future Systems would have hoped, and dragged out over two winters rather than just one. But the final result succeeds brilliantly. The air-conditioned disc hovers above the ground, an enigmatic, ambiguous form, whose scale and size are initially hard to read. It gives the television cameras an unimpeded view and the press a comfortable seat. It also signals the presence of Lords to passers-by. And the dramatic, glossy, curved shape of the centre has become familiar as a defining image for Lords, even though this last quality was never part of the brief.

The project led to Future Systems' design for the Selfridges department store in Birmingham (1999), the most striking part of a large new retail complex next to the city's main railway station, not least because the elliptical shape of the centre had caught the eye of Vittorio Radice, managing director of Selfridges at the time. A glimpse of the Media Centre from a passing car intrigued him enough to call Future Systems to discuss his plans for a new department store with them.

Radice revitalized and expanded Selfridges in the 1990s, starting with its original London store, by going back to the roots of the department store. Rather than pretending that Selfridges was just another out-of-town shopping mall that happened to occupy a city centre site, Radice played up the differences between a department store and other less flamboyantly theatrical forms of retailing.

When it was born in the nineteenth century, the department store was as much a social experience as a place to purchase functional necessities. The erosion of the city centre by affluent suburbs served to undermine the traditional department store. But as part of his strategy for revitalizing Selfridges, Radice reintroduced a sense of spectacle to retailing, in which architecture is an essential ingredient, just as it had been in the nineteenth century when Gordon Selfridge brought the great American architect Daniel Burnham to England and commissioned him to build a swaggering classical palazzo in Oxford Street.

When the developers came to offer his company space in what was still a drawing-board proposal, what attracted Radice most to the Birmingham project was the chance it allowed him to follow in the footsteps of Selfridge, and commission his own building. The developers offered to build Selfridges their own store and fit it out for their requirements, showing Radice the design they had in mind. Radice signed Selfridges up for space in the development, but insisted on a new design, and the appointment of his own architects to create it.

279 Selfridges Birmingham, department store, 1999.

279 Selfridges Birmingham,
department store, 1999.

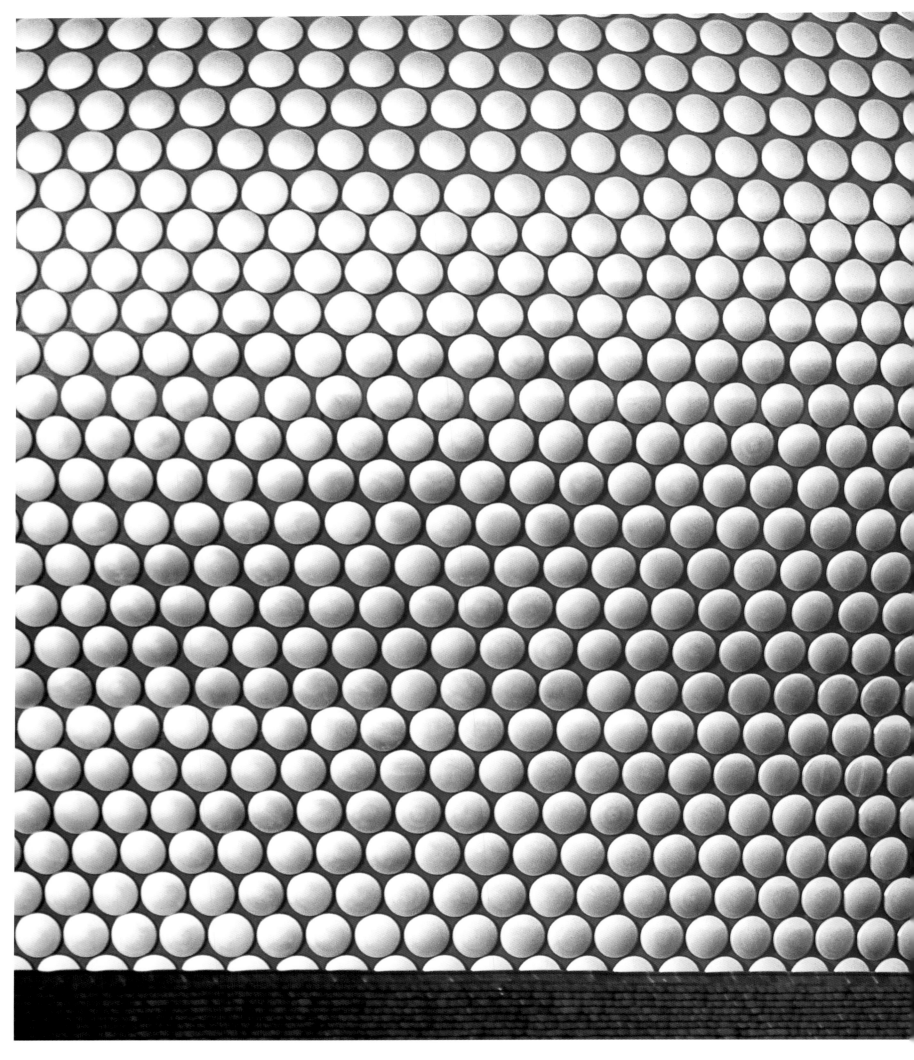

279 Selfridges Birmingham,
department store, 1999.

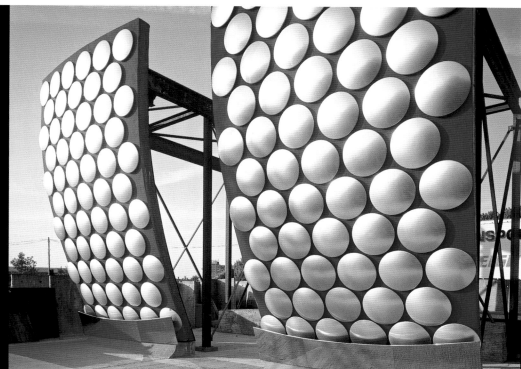

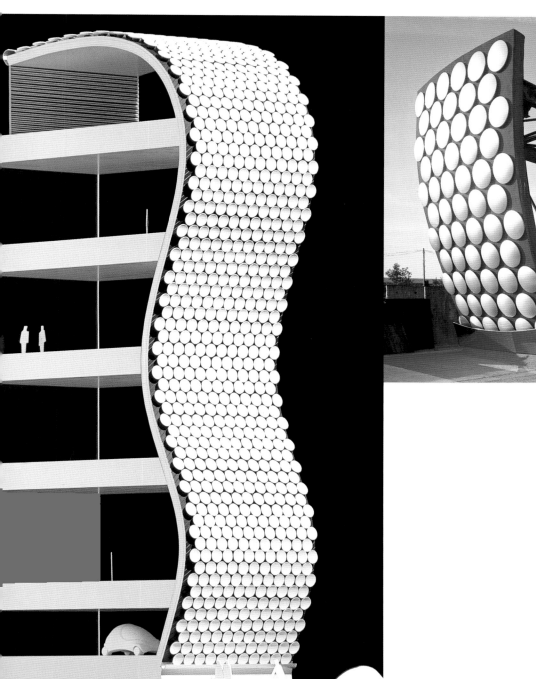

279 **Selfridges Birmingham,**
department store, 1999.

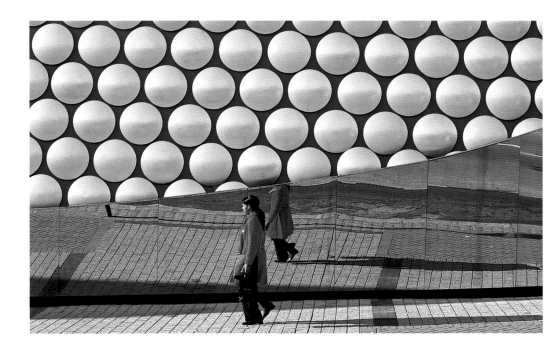

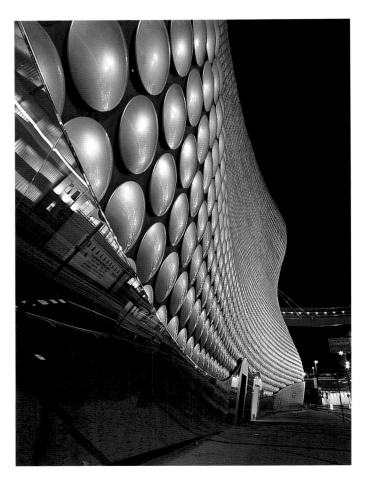

'We had a phone call out of the blue from Vittorio,' remembers Levete.

He had seen Lords and wanted to talk. He came to see us in our office, which was in Paddington in those days. There were just four people, and you could see that he'd thought we were going to be bigger. He started talking about the Birmingham project. The ambition was huge, but it had to be built for the same money as the conventional commercial version.

Somewhat to their surprise, Future Systems won an informal competition for the job. Their first thought was to build an entirely transparent store that would have been fully glazed. 'We thought that glimpses of people behind glass, and people moving up and down would have been a great draw, and the way to pull people in, but to do it, Selfridges believed that you would lose too much shopping space,' says Kaplicky. It is one of the continuing arguments about retailing, which can still be seen reverberating away even in the original Selfridges building, where most of the windows have been obscured over the years behind partitioning installed to provide extra display space, rather than, as it was thought, allowing daylight to distract shoppers from the matter at hand. Future Systems argued strongly that the Selfridges strategy should be to encourage shoppers to linger in the store as long as possible. This would involve

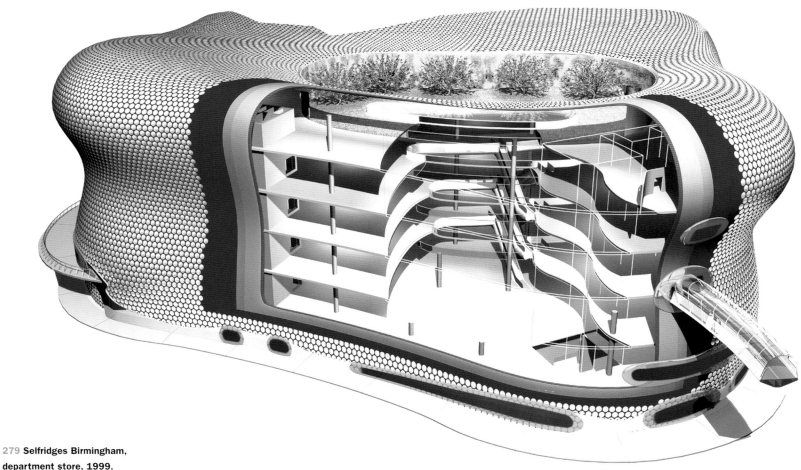

279 Selfridges Birmingham, department store, 1999.

filling the interior with daylight from the atrium and offering a series of generous cafés with views out over the city beyond the mall, as well as a roof garden, on the basis that, though it might be seen as a distraction from the impulse to consume, in the long run it would encourage people to spend more time and money in the store.

As it is, the curvaceous skin, 100 metres long, is punctuated at pavement level by stretched-glass openings that suggest wrap-around sunglasses. To make the store stand out throughout the day and night, each disc is individually lit, as well as bathed in the glow of floodlights mounted on the car park across the street. In addition, direct sunshine by day and the headlights of passing cars at night cause the building to sparkle.

Unlike Trafalgar Square, Birmingham's new shopping centre is a zone with an almost complete absence of architectural context. The store forms part of an aimless new shopping mall close to the railway station and adjacent to the Bull Ring street market. Next door is a florid Victorian gothic church and an isolated Pop Art circular tower block, known as the Rotunda. For Future Systems it was a site that demanded a building that could make its own context. 'There is no fabric,' says Kaplicky:

Well, there is a nineteenth-century church, which is fine, though it's just like sixteen others, and there is the Rotunda. The rest is the worst of the worst. I realized from the first site visit and looking at the view from the Rotunda, that there was the need for a building here that had the potential to be a landmark.

It became a classic iconic building in no time, **almost instantly,** almost by the next morning **Jan Kaplicky**

Future Systems' design looks as if it belongs to a different universe from the mall to which it is attached. At the top of the hill is the conventional, pastel-coloured neo-post-modernism of an utterly banal shopping centre. Selfridges erupts from one end to create an instantly recognizable landmark. It sits on the southern end of the site, tightly hemmed in by roads on the edge of high ground that rapidly falls away, making it highly conspicuous when viewed from the south.

Future Systems has built a giant blue bubble, studded with hundreds of anodized aluminium discs, that belongs to a family of objects relating to the work of such artists as Claes Oldenburg and Anish Kapoor. One image that provided a point of departure was an image of a dress designed in the 1960s by Paco Rabanne using a series of linked, polished-metal discs. But Selfridges is more than a sculptural object. It skilfully exploits changes of level and nuances of light and shade as they fall on the twisting contours of its surface. Its sweeping curves certainly create a sensational first impression. But the expectations aroused by the exterior are amply fulfilled by the interior, which is just as much a departure from the bland norms of retailing aesthetics as the exterior, while also alluding to the history of the grand department store. At the heart of Selfridges is a snow-white atrium, criss-crossed by escalators, and reached from the neighbouring car park by a Future Systems-designed pedestrian bridge. In fact it is two atria, one with a roof light that provides a sense of the weather outside. In a contemporary way, it recreates the splendours of Aristide Boucicault's Bon Marché in Paris, celebrated in Zola's novel *Bonheur de Dames*.

The building process was more straightforward than that of the Media Centre. Despite its complex form, it is achieved by relatively simple means. The precision of the shell of circular discs that gives Selfridges its form is underpinned by a much more forgiving supporting structure. A steel frame is wrapped in concrete sprayed onto a mesh base and finished with waterproof paint. Each of the 15,000 discs are supported on a single bolt cast into the concrete. Future Systems looked at various options for the outer skin. The idea of triangles, rather than discs was explored briefly. Work was done on the possibility of using ceramic discs, but they turned out to be too expensive. Tests and mock-ups were made to compare concave discs with the convex version that was eventually adopted. Levete explains:

> We set out the position of every disc on a drawing, but on site we had to adjust them, and we decided that spacing them so that the horizontal lines seemed to dominate looked better than vertical. We tried yellow as a background; we thought about coloured

discs. In the end we chose deep Yves Klein blue. We asked the Yves Klein Foundation for the exact pigment mix, but it turned out that it was designed for light-controlled interiors and in an outdoor environment would have faded within weeks, so we got as close as we could with waterproof, exterior-grade paint.

The discs are a rain screen rather than a waterproof structural layer, but the fixings are designed to be capable of carrying the weight of a man, in order to deal with potential unofficial abseilers. The architects even had to consider the possibility of nesting birds – regular hawk flights overhead are considered sufficient deterrent to discourage them.

Even before Selfridges opened, it had become enough of an icon for a graphic representation of its metal discs to be used, without further explanation needed, as an instantly recognizable symbol for the city. Selfridges' discs have become shorthand for the store, and thus for a new Birmingham, busy trying to shrug off its bleak, post-war image. At the time of the opening, the concourse at the city's main railway station, New Street, was dominated by a giant advertising hoarding promoting a local bank that used an abstracted image of the Selfridges discs as a means of instantly establishing its local credentials. It is a powerful example of the way in which architecture can be used to create a sense of identity for a whole city. 'When you design a simple object over a complex form, unexpected things happen. But it's better than you could have imagined,' says Levete. Kaplicky recalls Vittorio Radice asking him if he thought that the department store would need a sign, and replying that it would not be necessary. The architecture has taken on that role.

Future Systems' design for the new store was conceived by Radice from the outset as an important part of what would make the new Selfridges seem special. In Oxford Street, Burnham used a giant classical order to create a temple of consumerism that created an aura for the Selfridges name, effortlessly crushing its competitors through its scale and grandeur. Future Systems' curvaceous free-form blob in Birmingham conspicuously suggests that after a couple of decades of decline the department store, once again, had a contemporary relevance.

This was Future Systems' biggest project to be realized to date, and it depended on Levete's

The basic **idea** was **two buildings** that **did not look** **like** buildings

Jan Kaplicky

organizational skills and her appetite for engagement with the messy realities of the construction process, as well as the single-mindedness of Kaplicky's vision. With its apparently endless, rippling walls, the store is big not just in terms of scale, but also in the complexity of its range of uses, and the interactions with the large number of people who visit it. For Future Systems it was a confident demonstration of their ability to make a significant jump in size. If in some senses the Media Centre at Lords was a huge object, created using shipbuilding techniques, and reading as if it were an aircraft perched on a roof top, Selfridges has a more complex relationship with its setting. Its scale allows it to be experienced close up by pedestrians as they negotiate its threshold, but also as an element in the urban landscape by drivers passing by in their cars. It is a piece of design, as well as a work of architecture and urbanism, with its carefully planned creation of multilevel pedestrian routes through and around it.

Radice wanted to make a big, bold architectural gesture, but he was also careful to maintain a retailer's eye on the store. Rather than making the interior all of a piece with the exterior, Selfridges wanted to use a range of different designers to give a different identity to the various departments. In the end, Future Systems retained control of the key elements of the interior, the escalators, with their mix of matt GRC undersides and gloss GRP upper surfaces, the glass balustrades and the food hall at the foot of the elevators, to set the tone. The other floors were designed by Aldo Cibic, Eldrige Smerin and Stanton Williams.

In a department store, pride of place is traditionally given to the perfume and cosmetic departments, which are located by the main entrance, with floor space devoted increasingly to bigger, less profitable items in direct proportion to their distance from the door. In Selfridges Birmingham it is not so clear where the main entrance is. There are several points of entrance, from the mall as well as from the pedestrian bridge, which connects to the underground car park. In a sense, there is no ground floor. But the café and the restaurant are positioned on the top floor, while the food hall, which is not really a food hall, is at the base of the atrium, dispensing not conventional fresh foods, but chocolate, gifts and deli fare.

Future Systems are far from being professional icon builders, but their work has certainly prefigured many of the directions that a more demonstrative and formally inventive architecture has taken. They have had the courage to explore startlingly new forms and geometries ahead of the field. 'A building has to last. It can't just be about fashion,' says Kaplicky. But Selfridges opened the way to a period of even freer experimentation, as in the submission for the flawed competition to remodel London's South Bank cultural centre (2001), and in the construction of the Naples metro station. In both

305 South Bank, cultural centre, London, 2001.

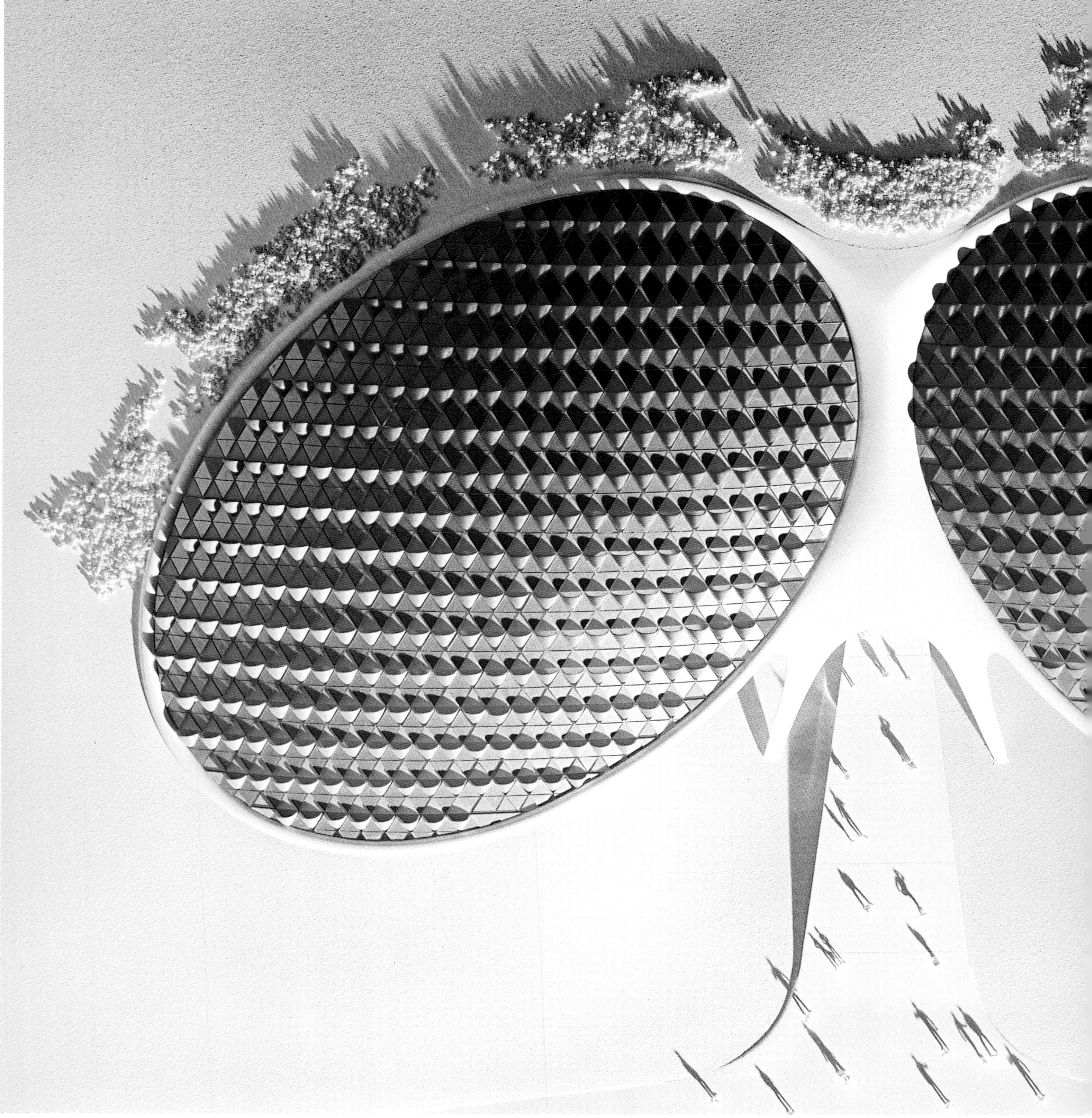

224 **Earth Centre, conference and education centre, Doncaster, 1995.**

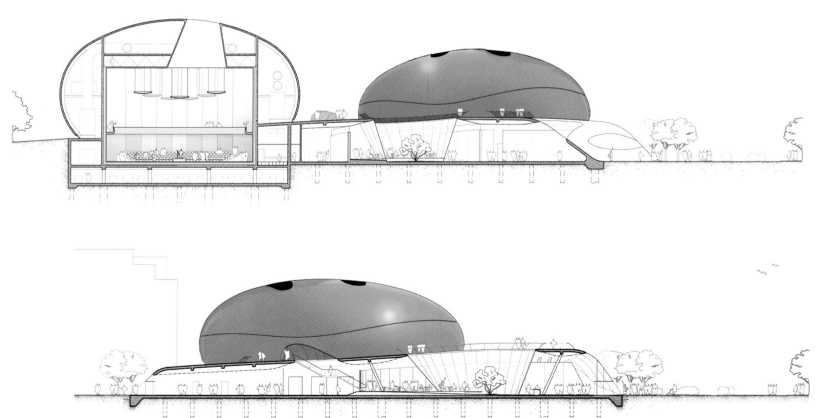

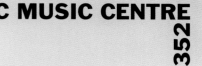

352 BBC Music Centre, London, 2003.

projects, the architects worked with the sculptor Anish Kapoor, and went on to cooperate with him on an unsuccessful submission for the competition for the Princess of Wales's memorial in Kensington Gardens.

The competition for the South Bank cultural centre resulted in something of a fiasco. The judges attempted to harness two incompatible architects, Rafael Vinoly and FOA, with disastrous results. But among the more intriguing submissions was the one from Kapoor and Future Systems. Rather than focusing on architectural detail, they put forward a strategy to deal with what they saw as the most pressing issues facing the site. They proposed a landscape rather than a building. A low, rounded artificial hillside would form the cultural building demanded by the brief, offset by a circular depression that would accommodate the commercial space needed to pay for the scheme. According to Future Systems:

> We tried a building that went down, and another that went up: a rough rectangle, with a sunken part that would have been an inward-looking gallery. Some of the forms would have been available to walk on, others not. The basic idea was two buildings that did not look like buildings.

As a landmark, it would have been powerful precisely because it was more a piece of landscape than an isolated object, a quality that runs through many of their projects, such as their design for the ill-fated Earth

Centre (1995), the failed eco-visitor attraction outside Doncaster. Future Systems' part of the complex could have provided the kind of instantly recognizable attraction that would have brought in visitors. But the Earth Centre decided to build a less challenging structure first, and perhaps in part as a result, closed for want of custom.

The religous building is of course the primary traditional landmark. The church, or any other kind of sacred building, is designed to be the largest and the most prominent building in so many different communities. In the secular western world, the position of the church as the physical and symbolic heart of the community is under threat. Commerce can build taller and bigger than the church. But the interest of religous groups in reminding the contemporary world of their values through architectural landmarks is as strong as ever, as demonstrated by Future Systems' work on the design of a church in Portugal. Intended for a suburban site, Kaplicky's preliminary studies explore the methods by which architecture can signal the sacred through form and iconography without referring to tradition.

In the wake of the success of Selfridges, Future Systems have found themselves increasingly in demand for high-profile projects. They took part in the BBC's competition for a music centre on the Television Centre campus at White City, London. Their design, a cluster of primary-coloured spheres, would have formed a gateway to the complex. They also took part, along with other

architects, in plans for the reconstruction of the derelict Battersea Power Station.

From Kaplicky's earliest sketches, to the famous montages, Future Systems have been associated with highly polished, sinuous objects, existing alone, or in landscapes, isolated from their surroundings. The speculative skyscrapers came close to the scale of a city, but they could not be called urban projects. It was only in 2005 that Future Systems addressed the idea of urban scale, with their master plan for the development of a strip of desert near Abu Dhabi's airport. It combines landmark structures with water and a monorail public-transport system to reduce car movements. At the centre is a cluster of towers, designed to accommodate a variety of functions with housing plots, retailing and social facilites ranged around them, the whole designed to soften the harshness of the desert heat.

Throughout their varied practice, Future Systems have proved themselves capable of working on the widest range of scales, from spoons to urban landscapes.

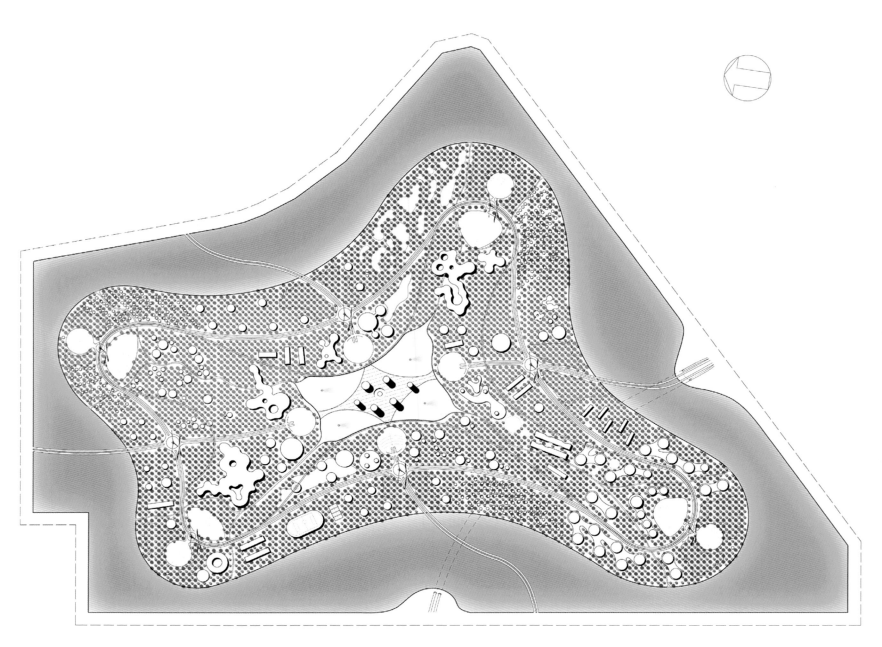

405 **Oasis City, master plan,
Abu Dhabi, 2005.**

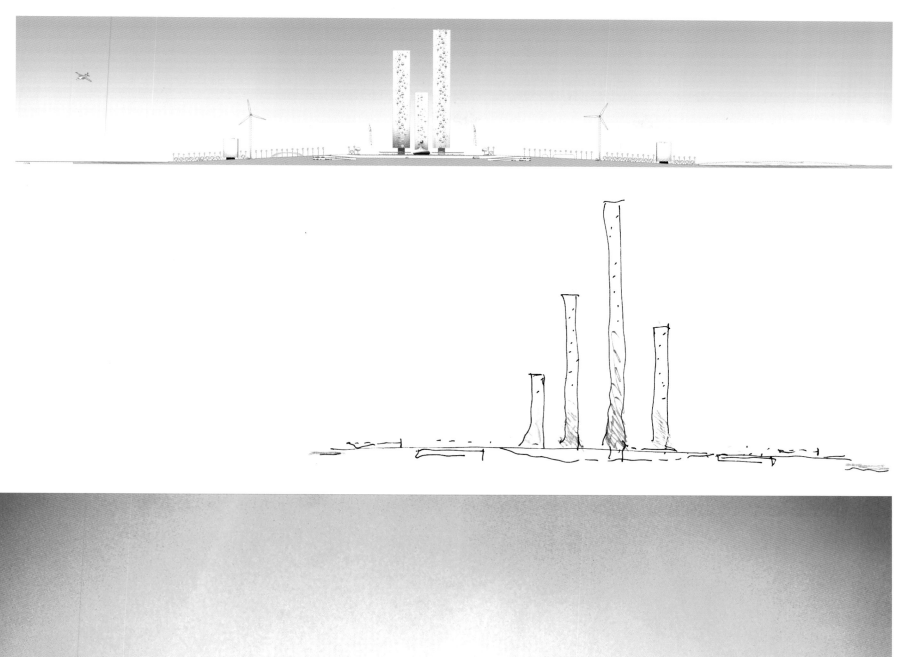

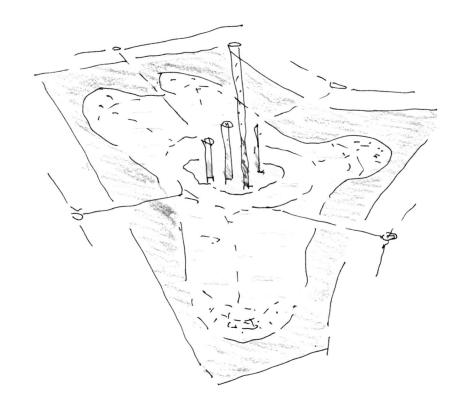

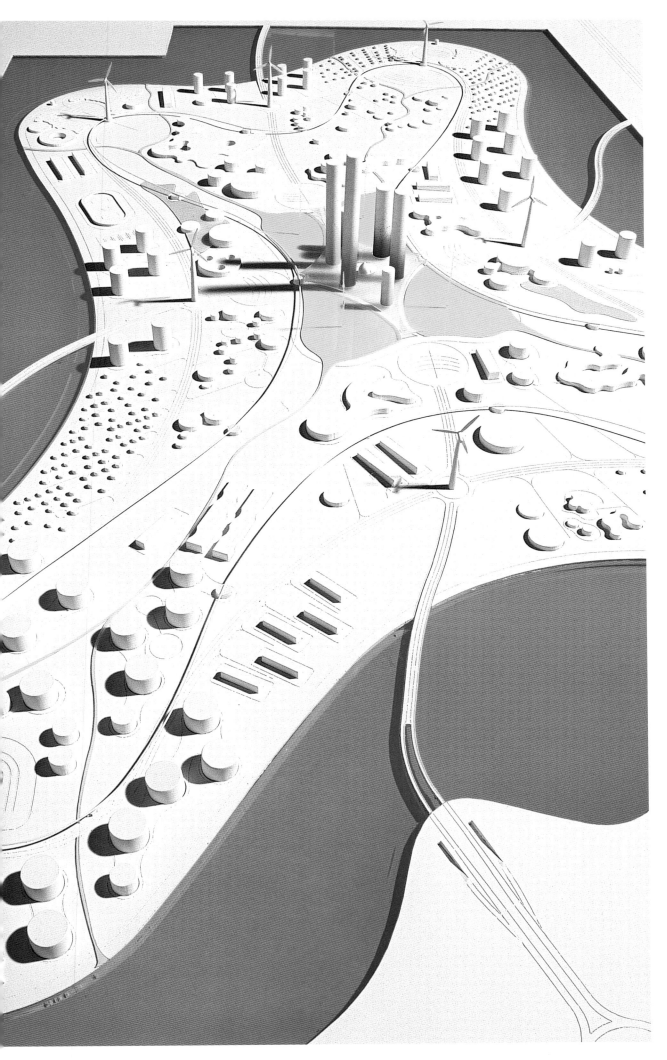

405 Oasis City, master plan,
Abu Dhabi, 2005.

CHRONOLOGY

Future Systems began in 1979 as a partnership between Jan Kaplicky (1937) and David Nixon (1947). For the next decade, the pair developed an impressive record of visionary projects that inspired a generation of architects and engineers. A new era began in 1989 when Amanda Levete (1955) joined Kaplicky as partner.

The buildings Future Systems have since realized have been award winning and seminal in their influence, including the Hauer King House, the Floating Bridge and the Lord's Media Centre, which received the Stirling Prize in 1999. Future Systems' extraordinary building for Selfridges in Birmingham opened in 2003. Current work includes a subway station in Naples, Italy in collaboration with the artist Anish Kapoor and the new Maserati Museum in Modena, Italy.

Future Systems' competition work, from projects such as the New Acropolis Museum and the Bibliothèque de France to the Hallfield School Prototype, are equally influential. A commitment to research is a vital part of the practice's philosophy. Projects such as Green Building, Green Bird and Project ZED, an investigation into zero energy buildings, have been applauded and copied in equal measure.

Jan Kaplicky was born in Prague in 1937 where he studied to become an architect. He has lectured in more than twenty countries around the world, has written nine books and has been published in over thirty countries to date.

Amanda Levete trained at the Architectural Association and worked for Richard Rogers before joining Future Systems. She contributes to a number of publications and is a regular broadcaster as well as a trustee of Art Angel and the Architecture Foundation.

The coloured numbers in this chronology indicate the project codes used throughout the book

BIBLIOGRAPHY

Monographs on Future Systems

Jan Kaplicky with a foreword by Zaha
Hadid, *Sketches* (Prague, Fraktaly
Publishers, 2005)

Ivan Margolias and Jan Kaplicky,
Czech Inspiration (Prague, Fraktaly
Publishers, 2005)

Jan Kaplicky, *Jan Kaplicky Album* (Prague,
Labyrint, 2005)

Future Systems, (Prague, Zlatý Rez, 2002)

Jan Kaplicky, *Confessions* (London, Wiley,
2002)

Paul Finch, *Unique Building: Lord's Media
Centre* (London, Wiley, 2001)

Marcus Field, *Future Systems* (London,
Phaidon Press, 1999)

Jan Kaplicky, *More For Inspiration Only*
(London, Academy Editions, 1999)

Martin Pawley, *Future Systems: Hauer King
House* (London, Phaidon Press, 1997)

Jan Kaplicky, *For Inspiration Only* (London,
Academy Editions, 1996)

Martin Pawley, *Future Systems: The Story of
Tomorrow* (London, Phaidon Press, 1993)

Ron Herron, *Future Systems* (London,
Architectural Association, 1987)

Books that feature work by Future Systems

Ian Luna, *Retail: Architecture and Shopping*
(New York, Rizzoli, 2005)

Ana Canizares, *Great New Buildings of the
World: Works from Tadao Ando to Zaha Hadid*
(New York, Harper Design, 2005)

Lance Fung, ed., *The Snow Show* (London,
Thames & Hudson, 2005)

Dominic Bradbury, *New Country House*
(London, Laurence King, 2005)

Matthew Wells, *Skyscrapers: Structure
and Design* (London, Laurence King, 2005)

Peter Hyatt, *Design With Glass: Great Glass
Buildings* (Melbourne, Images Publishing
Group, 2004)

Kester Rattenbury, Rob Bevan and Kieran
Long, *Architects Today* (London, Laurence
King, 2004)

Sophie Flouquet, *L'Architecture
Contemporaine* (Paris, Editions Scala, 2004)

Phaidon Press Editors, *The Phaidon Atlas of
Contemporary World Architecture* (Phaidon
Press, London, 2004)

Kenneth Powell, *New Architecture in Britain*
(Merrell, London, 2003)

Christian Schittich, ed., *Building in Existing
Fabric: Refurbishment, Extensions, New
Designs* (Birkhauser, Basel, 2004)

Sutherland Lyall, *Masters of Structure:
Engineering Today's Innovative Buildings*
(Laurence King, London, 2002)

Jan Kaplicky, ed., *Looking Back in Envy*
(Academy, London, 2001)

Kenneth Powell, *New London Architecture*
(Merrell, London, 2001)

Martin Pawley, ed., *Fashion and Architecture*
(Academy, London, 2000)

Ivan Margolius, *Automobiles by Architects*
(Wiley-Academy, London, 2000)

Olivier Boissiere, *Twentieth-Century Houses:
Europe* (Editions Pierre Terrail, Paris, 1998)

Peter Murray and Mary Anne Stevens, eds.,
*Living Bridges: The Inhabited Bridge, Past,
Present and Future* (Prestel, New York, 1996

Articles

'Hot Desks', *Evening Standard Magazine*
(London, 2006)

'The Italian Job', *The Independent Magazine*
(London, 2006)

'Stazione Metropolitana Monte Sant'Angelo',
Casabella (Milan, 2006)

'Feature: Architects Offices', *A+U* (Tokyo,
2006)

'Best of British', *The Times* (London, 2005)

'Naples Embraces Future', *Building Design*
(London, 2005)

'Mise en Boule', *Vogue Paris* (Paris, 2005)

'A new look for Birmingham', *The Guardian*
(London, 2005)

'Selfridges Birmingham from the inside', *A+U*
(Tokyo 2005)

'Nouveau look pour New Look', *Architecture
Intérieur Crée* (Paris, 2005)

'Future Systems', *Icon* (London, 2005)

'Selfridges Birmingham', *Arup Journal* (London, 2005)

'Maserati Museum', *The Architects' Journal* (London 2005)

'House in Wales, Hauer King House', *Interior World* (London, 2004)

'New Look for New Look', *A+U* (Tokyo, 2004)

'Radar: Amanda Levete', *Building Design* (London 2004)

'…Curvaceous outpost in Birmingham…', *Architectural Record* (New York, 2004)

'Birmingham (Royaume-Uni) Une icone pour la ville', *Le Moniteur* (Paris, 2004)

'My first Vogue moment', *Vogue* (London, 2004)

'Space Ship Selfridges', *Metropolis* (New York, 2004)

'Holiday House in Wales', *L'industria delle costruzioni* (Rome, 2003)

'New Look shapes up', *The Guardian* (London 2003)

'Future Systems' Selfridges', *Casa Brutus* (Tokyo 2003)

'Back to the future', *Elle* (London, 2003)

'Urban Icon', *Domus* (Milan, 2003)

'Selfridges', *The Independent* (London, 2003)

'The wait is finally over', *The Birmingham Post* (Birmingham, 2003)

'Department store in Birmingham', *Detail* (Munich, 2003)

'What's new?', *Vogue* (London, 2003)

'Unique selling point', *The Sunday Times* (London, 2003)

'Confessions', *Axis* (Tokyo, 2002)

'La Biennale di Venezia', *Domus* (Milan, 2002)

'Future Systems', *Stavba* (Prague, 2002)

'Green Architecture', *Architectural Design* (London, 2001)

'Comme Des Garçons/Green Bird', *Playboy Slovenia* (Ljubljana, 2001)

'Future Shop', *The New York Times Magazine* (New York, 2001)

'Fashion Shop in London', *Detail* (Munich, 2001)

'House in Wales by Future Systems', *Dwell* (San Francisco, 2001)

'Future Systems: An Identity for Marni's Clothes', *Domus* (Milan, 2000)

'Birmingham Selfridges Building', *Design Week* (London, 2000)

'Selfridges goes to Birmingham', *The Sunday Times* (London, 2000)

'Pedestrian Bridge, West India Dock, London', *Detail* (Munich, 1999)

'Organique et fluide', *L'architecture d'aujourd'hui* (Paris, 1999)

'Stirling Prize', *Architects Journal* (London, 1999)

'Vogue Architecture – Jan Kaplicky', *Vogue Italia* (Milan, 1999)

'Future Systems', *L'architecture d'aujourd'hui* (Paris, 1999)

'Into the Future', *Vogue* (London, 1999)

'Lord's spaceship has landed', *The Times* (London, 1999)

'Comme des Garçons Tunnel', *Architects Journal* (London, 1999)

'Josef K House', *Blueprint* (London, 1999)

'Come Back Jan Kaplicky', *Stavba* (Prague,1999) 'Future Systems', *Zlaty Rez* (Prague, 1998)

FUTURE SYSTEMS TEAM 1979–2006

SOREN AAGAARD

LINDY AITKIN

VOLKAN ALKANOGLU

ANGELA BARDENS

NERIDA BERGIN

SHEELAH BOOKATZ

FEDERICO CELONI

LIDA CHARSOULI

SHEEMA CHAUHAN

JAKUB CIGLER

JONATHON CLARK

FERNANDA CURI

TAMSYN CURLEY

HELENE DAHER

DESIREE DAVIS

ALAN DEMPSEY

SAM DONNELLY

ERBAY ERTUGRUL

GERALDINE FOURMON

ADRIAN FOWLER

JULIAN FLANNERY

JORDY FU

HARVINDER GABHARI

CHRIS GENESTE

KATY GHAVEMANI

ROBIN GILL

CRISTINA GRECO

DOMINIC HARRIS

NICOLA HAWKINS

ROSY HEAD

MATTHEW HEYWOOD

FILIP JACOBS

SARAH JAYNE BOWEN

CANDAS JENNINGS

JAN KAPLICKY

NICOLA KIRKMAN

MISHA KITLEROVA

HIDEO KUMAKI

CY LAU

BILLY LEE

AMY LEUNG

AMANDA LEVETE

IAIN MacKAY

NICHOLAS MANSOUR

CLANCY MEARS

LIZ MIDDLETON

DAVID MILLER

MIKE MITCHELL

GLENN MOORLEY

JEFF MORGAN

ANDREA MORGANTE

MARK NEWTON

YANINA ANDREA NICASTRO

DAVID NIXON

PERNILLA OHRSTEDT

JOHN O'MARA

RICARDO OSTOS

THORSTEIN OVERBERG

ITAI PALTI

IRIS PAPADATOU

MARIA PERSICHELLA

CARLOTTA POGGIARONI

ANGUS POND

PETER RICHARDSON

REBECCA RICHWHITE

LIZ ROOT

FAROOQ SABIR

THEO SARANTOGLOU

ERIC TONG

BUKKY SALAMI

JESSICA SALT

SEVERIN SODER

RACHEL STEVENSON

ANTHONY ST LEGER

ADRIAN THOMPSON

LIZ WESTGARTH

ARTURO VITTORI

SHEAN YU

INDEX

ACKNOWLEDGEMENTS

2D 3D
A Models
Adams Kara Taylor
Arup
Atelier One
Bakers Patterns
BDSP Partnership
Billings Design Associates
Boyden & Co
Brian Clarke
Buro Happold
Richard Davies
Faggionato Fine Arts
Forum
Diego Garcia Scaro
Antony Gormley
Anthony Hunt Associates
Zaha Hadid
Josef Kaplicky
Anish Kapoor
Davis Langdon
Lee Associates
Lovejoy

Mott MacDonald
Dewhurst MacFarlane
Ann Minogue
Network
Pierandrei Associati
Politecnia
Ken Powell
Savant
Richard Schlagman
Martha Schwartz Partners
Mike Sindic
Sound and Space Design
Strasky Husty S.R.O
Studio Legale Corabi
Suburbia
Deyan Sudjic
Techniker
Emilia Terragni
Townshend Landscape Architects
Unit 22
Vogt Landscape Architects
Sarah Wedderburn

Picture credits

The pictures in this book belong to the archive of Future Systems, except where noted. All reasonable efforts have been made to trace the copyright holders of images. We apologize to anyone that we have been unable to contact.

Soren Aagaard 22, 23. 30, 31, 32, 33, 34, 35, 38–9, 42, 44, 52, 53, 67, 68, 69, 92–3, 98 (b), 99, 100, 106–7, 108, 109, 132 (t), 133, 165, 166, 167, 170 (l), 171 (l), 196 (cr), 197, 202, 204–5, 206, 207 (b), 208 (t), 212–3, 229; Alessi 8–9, 18–19; Richard Bryant 46; Richard Davies 11, 12, 13. 14–15, 20-1, 26–7, 48, 49, 54, 55, 56, 57, 74, 75 (t), 76, 77, 78, 79 (t), 80, 81, 84, 85, 86 (tr), 87, 102–3, 114–5, 117, 118 (b), 119, 124, 125, 132 (t), 133, 134, 135 (b), 138–9, 140–1, 143 (t), 145 (b), 146, 147, 148–9, 155, 156, 159, 162, 178–9, 181 (t), 182–3, 184, 185, 188, 189 (t), 189 (br), 191, 192–3, 200–1, 203, 207 (t), 209, 210, 211, 214–5, 216–7, 218–9, 220, 221; Jeffrey Debany 101; Masa Yuki Mayashi 70, 71; Andrea Morgante 88 (b), 89 (t); Royal Mail 240

Phaidon Press Limited
Regent's Wharf
All Saints Street
London N1 9PA

Phaidon Press Inc.
180 Varick Street
New York, NY 10014

www.phaidon.com

First published 2006
© 2006 Phaidon Press Limited

ISBN-10: 0 7148 4469 1
ISBN-13: 9 780 7148 4469 5

A CIP Catalogue record for this
book is available from the
British Library

Designed by Suburbia
Printed in China